SECRETS OF LANDING THE JOB

SECRETS OF LANDING THE JOB

How to identify your true value and position yourself as the candidate of choice.

By
Holly Sweat Raper
James Jennings

Copyright © 2019
Holly Sweat Raper & James Jennings

Publishing Services by Happy Self Publishing
www.happyselfpublishing.com

Year: 2019

All rights reserved. No reproduction, transmission or copy of this publication can be made without the written consent of the author in accordance with the provision of the Copyright Acts. Any person doing so will be liable to civil claims and criminal prosecution.

Happy Self Publishing.

Acknowledgments

I'd like to say a special thank you to

James Jennings.

James made this project a reality. People have asked me for years to write a book, and without him, this book would have never been written.

I am eternally grateful!

* * *

To **Mason** and **Taylor,** my twins.

Thank you for believing in me and encouraging me to speak and write.

I love you!

TABLE OF CONTENTS

Acknowledgments 5

Introduction 9

Chapter One: Let's Bake Something 13

Chapter Two: The 5 Secrets of Landing The Job 17

Chapter Three: Barriers & Blunders 25

Chapter Four: The Cover Letter: Make The Proper (Effective) First Impression ... 35

Chapter Five: The Dynamic Resume: Getting the Interview 41

Chapter Six: Listing References 57

Chapter Seven: Polish and Proofread 61

Chapter Eight: Putting it Together 65

Chapter Nine: Examining Different Types of Resumes 75

Chapter Ten: Beyond the Resume 95

Chapter Eleven: Acing the Interview 101

Chapter Twelve: The Power of Networking 109

Final Thoughts: Where Can You Make a Difference? 125

Recommendations 127

Awards 137

Thank You ! 139

INTRODUCTION

The Secrets of Landing The Job conveys a powerful message of possibility, opportunity, and action that has helped create startling and powerful change over thousands of individuals' lives as they learn to successfully navigate through the maze of employment opportunities. Secrets of Landing the Job reveals a paradigm shift on how you see yourself, your career, and the value you offer. You will read real-life stories about individuals who successfully implemented these strategies and found success in their career goals. Designed to give you practical tools to magnify your highest good, this information inspires you to transform your unconscious habits into conscious actions that will create success in life and success in your career. The three key takeaways in this book are:

- Learning the 5 Secrets of Employment Success
- The importance of a GREAT first impression: A Dynamic Resume, LinkedIn Profile, and a 30 Second Commercial
- Understanding the Hidden Job Market.

It Doesn't have to be Hard
If you know the Secrets

As I mentioned, I have worked with thousands of people in my career: welders, nurses, engineers, executives, and students, just to name a few. The common denominator with all these people is they feel frustrated and overwhelmed and don't know where to begin or what to do. The information I teach gives them effective strategies for success. These strategies can work with anyone; in fact, let me share a story with you:

When I first arrived in Greenville, North Carolina, I was asked if I would teach a class at the community college. Yet, most everything in life comes with a catch, and this wonderful employment opportunity was no different. The class was basically *How to Get a Job 101: For Convicted Felons*. Yes, these guys were criminals, known gang members with multiple felonies, and their job *'skills,'* though eye-catching, were not exactly what one looks for on a resume, but they were trying. Still, it wasn't the most prestigious job on campus, and the chances of success were slim, so I wouldn't blame you for thinking that I was less than excited about the opportunity. Nothing could be further from the truth!

God makes all kinds of people and gifts them for all kinds of challenges, and He gifted me for this one. Early in my career, I had worked at a maximum-security detention center for juveniles. Here I met with young men with names like Snake and Spider who were incarcerated for such things as arson, rape, and even murder. So when they asked me to teach guys who had already made the effort to earn their welding credentials and various other work-related certifications at a community college, I said, "Where do I sign up?"

Still, these men were not going to find a job by simply applying online. Job training and a couple of certifications were not going to be enough to overcome their obstacles. What these men needed was training on how to get the job! So our goal (teacher and student) was to turn them into **competent job seekers** by educating them on the *5 Secrets to Landing a Job*.

After the completion of the course, one young man decided to try Secret #5, "Who does what I do?" Having worked in construction, he showed up to a worksite at 5:30 on a Monday morning ready for work. He knew from experience that it was not unusual for crews to be shorthanded because workers were prone to party a little too hard on the weekends. So, once there, my student finds the foreman of the job, introduces himself, and offers his services by giving his short *30-second commercial*.

"Are you looking for help?" he asks, "I am getting my degree in Welding at Pitt Community College. I just finished my OSHA 10 and my CRC and would love to help you in any way I can."

The foreman, short on workers and long on work, asks my student if he has any construction experience. Now the student is engaged in a real job interview with someone who can make a hiring decision. He tells the foreman that he has worked some residential construction for a man in his church doing things like sheetrock, laying pipe, and working with power tools. The foreman says, "Great, I can use you. Go fill out an application in the trailer so we can get you started."

Job secured; Mission completed!

Okay, I know the little voice in your head is screaming, "It's not that easy! What about his record?" Well, you are right. The felonies needed to be addressed.

"Sir, I want to be honest with you." The student went on, "I have felonies, but that's behind me. I am trying to change my life, which is why I am in school working on my certifications. If you give me a chance, I promise I will show up early, work late, and you can drug test me every day." The foreman hired him.

As for it being that easy, it was. The student put in the hard work to learn and develop quality job skills and then went the extra mile to learn *how to land* the job. After that, getting the job is just a matter of applying what you've learned. Sure, whether you have a Ph.D. or a long distinguished criminal record, finding a job can be scary, but that doesn't mean that it is hard. It just means that someone needs to turn on the light for you. There are secrets, things that most people don't know, to landing a job, but over the next few chapters, my goal is to share these secrets with you so that you can find the perfect spot to do what *you* do best!

I realize people get so disheartened when looking for a job. Through these chapters, you will be reminded you have VALUE, you have skills, you just need to articulate what you have done so people have a clear understanding of what you can do. Through the years, my clients have said I not only gave them tools and strategies, I gave them HOPE!

Chapter One

Let's Bake Something

I confess, I have binged watched my fair share of Cupcake Wars. It's a guilty pleasure. Yet, it is an extremely popular show, and it's not the only competitive baking show on television. "Why?" you wonder. I think that it's because, for most people, baking is still very much akin to magic. It both intrigues and frightens the average person. Yet, there are people, like those on these reality shows, that do it so well. How?

The key is that they understand what they are trying to accomplish, and they know how to accomplish it. *Success* never happens by accident, it takes planning. The old adage is, "You have to know what you want, know when you want it, and most importantly, you need to know what it will take to get it."

For the bakers covered in dough, frantically searching for the marmalade to add to their frosting concoction, the end goal is the perfect $25,000 winning cupcake. Since you are investing your time reading this book, it is a safe bet that your desire is to gain employment and not just any job. You want *THE job*.

So how do we accomplish that goal? We make Cupcakes! Okay, not really, but the principle is the same. Remember, baking may look like magic, and it may seem very hard, and that may frighten us, but the truth is that baking is as simple as following directions.

You see, the key to reaching your goal lies in understanding what it takes to produce the end results.

Certain steps must be followed, and certain ingredients must be used to land the job that you desire. If you skip a step or leave out an ingredient while you are mixing your cupcake batter, you will be disappointed with what comes out of the oven. The same thing can be said for our job search.

Tip: *Read the directions and never try to shortcut the process. This is how we end up missing out on the right job and, worse yet, being hired for the wrong one.*

So let's look at the recipe for Landing Your Next Job.

Ingredient #1: Communication

As a psychotherapist for over 20 years, my expertise lies in communication. I love to talk with people, and I learned early on that the secret to communication is saying things in a way that a person can receive it. It's not what you say but **how** you say it that makes it effective.

Yet, often, when we speak about ourselves, we come across pessimistic and even a bit negative, especially when we are searching for our next job. **The Secrets of Landing The Job** provides you with strategies that help you communicate your value and worth in a way that people will receive. The right words spoken in the right way are empowering, motivating, and inspiring. They allow people to see the potential that your experience, education, and drive will add to their team.

Tip: *Remember Negativity is Natural, Positivity is Powerful.*

Ingredient #2: Understand Who You Are

If you are going to communicate your value, then it is important for you to Understand Who You Are.

Knowing who you are means knowing what you want and where you want to go. Direction is based on knowing who you are and what you like, knowing what you're good at, even what you don't like. All of these help you figure out what you want to in your life and career. *If your Career is an extension of yourself, it is imperative that you know yourself.* We can't talk about where you want to work if you don't even know what you like or what you are good at. And I promise, saying you just want a job will not get you where you want to go! That's like saying you are going on vacation, then when asked, "Where are you going?" You say, "I don't know." Well how will you know when you get there? You have to at least have an idea of the destination, or you will just drift through life without ever discovering your purpose and what makes you happy.

Perhaps even more crucial is recognizing that your circumstance of being **UNEMPLOYED** is not *who you are*. For many, the state of being unemployed is a frightening and unsettling experience. It is critical to remember that being unemployed does not wipe away your experience, it does not invalidate your education, nor does it reflect poorly on your work ethic. Being unemployed simply means that you are between employers.

If you are a qualified electrician, lifeguard, schoolteacher, or a day laborer, then that is what you are regardless of whether someone is currently paying you for those services. What you never say is that you are **UNEMPLOYED.** Remember, you are communicating your *value* to potential employers!

Employed or unemployed tells someone your current *employment status*, but what they need to know is, **"What do you do?"** That is an entirely different question, and it conveys your potential value to them.

This is important enough that I am going to say it again. When someone asks you, "So what do you do?" the answer is NEVER, "I am unemployed." That is your circumstance, NOT who you are.

In the process of searching for a job, whether you were fired, laid off, downsized, or just looking to transition to a different field, there is a danger of losing sight of your value. Therefore, once someone is no longer employed, it is not uncommon for them to experience a traumatic identity crisis. This is understandable, but it is also a product of 'wrong' thinking.

Here is where we make our paradigm shift or where we fix our thinking. It is true that people draw a sense of identity and even purpose from what they do. However, it is vital that we realize that there is a difference between what we do and who employs us. It is in this minute difference that we are able to recognize that our value does not reside in who employs us but rather in the skills, education, and experience that we possess and that we take those qualities with us when we change jobs.

When we are navigating the waters of unemployment, it is easy to panic and take on the 'I need your help because I am unemployed' mentality. In this state, we may desperately cling to whatever life preserver of a job that we can get our hands on. This is not a good job search strategy.

There needs to be a shift if we are to be successful. Rather than panic, let's develop a plan. Plans are always more effective and ultimately more rewarding than panic in the long run. Panic screams, "I need your help," but a plan states, "I have talent and expertise that can help you, and oh, by the way, I am available."

Ingredient #3: Follow a Proven Plan

The power is in the results. Persuasive words are just words unless there are results from those words. Even though, by some accounts, I am charismatic, and my presentations are inspiring and motivational, the strength of my presentations lies in their results. I have worked with thousands of people who have found jobs by applying the information that I teach.

Information with application leads to transformation.

A recent survey from NC Works in Pitt County (the employment office) found that 98% of students who completed the material I taught began interviewing within 2 weeks; 54% found a job within a month, and 87% found a job within 3 months.

The people I work with vary in their education, economic status, age and experience, and come from all walks of life, including CEO's, Human Resource Directors, Sale people, manufacturing, engineers, nurses, IT, cashiers, and yes even felons. Everyone needs and wants a job, and most everyone has the same question, "How do I find it?"

Please know, I don't want you to just find a job, but I want you to find Your Job.

Chapter Two

The 5 Secrets of Landing The Job

Information with Application leads to Transformation; *Knowledge is useless unless you apply it.* The 5 Secrets that I am about to share with you are life-transforming! However, if you just take in the information but do not apply the strategies, you will not get the results. Let me explain what I mean with this statement, "Information with Application leads to Transformation." We all realize that just knowing something does not mean you will have any results. EXAMPLE: I know a lot about losing weight. I know the importance of eating fewer calories and making sure those calories are a healthy combination of protein, fruits & vegetables, fiber, and healthy fats. I KNOW to drink at least eight 8-ounce glasses of water daily and the importance of exercise. However, even though I KNOW these things about diet, exercise, water, and even sleep, that does not mean I will get the results I am looking for. I might have every healthy cookbook in my kitchen, I could have a gym membership and a treadmill sitting in my living room. But if I am sitting on my couch eating a Twinkie and watching TV and NOT applying the information I know, then there will be NO transformation. The Secrets I'm about to reveal to you are to be applied. Just knowing some things and even understanding them will not get you the results you desire. It is applying the information that will lead to the transformation.

We take in a constant barrage of information from social media, 24-hours news channels, our well-meaning relatives... it comes from everywhere. What is amazing is how much of it we never actually use. It is just information with no application, and therefore, it has no significant effect on our lives.

The Secrets I'm about to share with you are Life Transforming. These Secrets or Strategies will not only change how people see you but how you view yourself. Proverbs says, "As a man thinks in his heart, so is he." We have heard for years this self-fulfilling prophecy. Well, it is true. Perception is Reality. Get ready for a Paradigm Shift that has transformed 1,000s of people's lives.

Secret #1: Never say, *"I'm unemployed looking for a job."* Folks, that is not who you are, it is just your current circumstance, and it will change! Saying that you are unemployed does not express your real value or what you have to offer. Telling someone your circumstance is useless. No employer cares what your circumstance is, in fact, saying you're unemployed, you might as well put a Big "L" for Loser on your forehead, because that is what that statement conveys, but it is NOT THE TRUTH. You are not a loser (even if you feel that way, your feelings are wrong). You have skills, abilities, experience, and education. Just because you are not currently receiving a paycheck does not mean you do not have value. So STOP putting an emphasis on your circumstance, and redirect people to what is important;

Who you are and what you have done. You have Skills, Abilities, and Experience!

Secret #2: *Know your 30-Second Commercial/ Elevator Speech.* You should be ready, when someone asks you to "Tell me about yourself," to give them the good stuff, the kind of stuff that makes you 'sexy' to a potential employer. It's no time to trip and stumble over words and spit out something about being married with children. Employers aren't interested in your kids, not really. They are interested in your skills and experience, so do them and yourself a favor, and be ready to tell them.

Name, rank, and serial number soldier! Who are you, what can you do, where have you done it... just the facts. The best predictor of the Future is the Past, so let employers know who you are, what you have done, where you have worked, your accomplishments, passion, strengths.

Secret #3: Get into the habit of saying, *"I'm currently looking at several opportunities."* Folks, you ARE looking at several opportunities; they do not need to know that those opportunities have not called you back. People want people that other people want. This is human nature. Be confident in what you have done and what you have to offer. Remember, don't define yourself by your current circumstance but rather by your SKILLS, ABILITIES, AND EXPERIENCE. The details of your employment are not relevant, nor are they attractive.

Let me emphasize again; The reality is, "people want people that other people want." That is why saying, "I'm currently looking at several opportunities," is effective. It creates an image in their mind that you are attractive and potentially about to be unavailable because someone else is going to get you. It's called creating a sense of urgency and demand... and yes, remember, you do have something to offer. People will automatically see you as having value, others want you. Then if they ask, "who are you talking to?" You can tell them; they are not going to call that employer and check. Now remember, the next time somebody asks, "Have you found a job yet?" refrain from engaging in physical violence and then say it again, "Actually, I'm currently looking at several opportunities."

You guys, I want you saying that phrase over and over again. Practice in your car, say it out loud, under your breath, constantly. Until it becomes a habit. Then when someone asks you what you are currently doing, or if you have found a job yet, you will automatically say, "Actually, I am currently looking at several opportunities." That is the one phrase I want you to highlight. I want you to put a star on it. I want you to write it on your wall. Most of all, I want you saying it! If you start saying, "I'm currently looking at several opportunities," several things will begin to happen.

One: it leads to further conversation.
Two: It says, "I have value."

You will not believe how different you feel when you respond that way and how it changes the way people react to you. People respond to how you make them feel. The reason Chick-fil-A is number one in Customer Service is because of how they make people feel, and they do that with what they say. Instead of saying, "You're welcome," they say, "It was my pleasure to serve you." They make you feel important. By saying, "You are currently looking at several opportunities," you are conveying that you HAVE VALUE, and you are exploring who could use it. What we say matters.

Faith goes a long way: I've had people say, "Holly, I am depressed, and it's hard to pretend I'm positive all the time."

Believe me, I understand. Transitioning is almost always difficult, even when we are going into something better. Sometimes though, it is a matter of believing something that we can't see or feel; for me, it's a matter of faith. It takes a certain amount of faith to believe that you have value when no one is paying you for your skills and abilities. I've been there.

A young boy once asked his dad where the stars went during the day. "Nowhere," the father replied.

You see, faith is not losing sight of the truth that the stars are there even though you can only see them at night. Unemployment is kind of like daytime; the skills and abilities are still there as sure as the stars hang in the heavens. You'll see.

The danger is that we can be our own worst critic. There can be many 'little' voices in your head shouting about bills, late notices, missed opportunities; it's enough to keep you up at night. So, for me, it has to begin here… in my heart. Especially when the critical voice in your head just gets to be too loud, you have to listen to something louder than you.

Now, I talk about God a great deal. I do. I admit it. It motivates me. If you don't believe, it's okay, but then what inspires you? Everybody needs to draw strength from somewhere.

I have to tell you, I had a gentleman in my class who proudly professed to be an atheist. One day, he said quite sincerely, "Holly, just because we are in the South doesn't mean we are all Christians."

Fair enough, but since he was in the South, he was surely outnumbered. The funny thing is one of the other people in the class looked at him up and down and said, "Oh, I've never seen an atheist before." It was at this moment that I was sure I had lost control of the class, and there would soon be flying chairs and lawsuits to follow.

"Sir, you are right," I responded. "However, this is how I get through life's battles, and I've gone through a lot in my life. But if I'm wrong, I've had a lifetime of hope, and then I die. If I'm right, I've had a lifetime of hope, and I then I get to live forever in paradise. Either way, it's a win-win." You see, it's not what you go through, but how you go through it that is important, and really, it's all that you can control anyway.

How are you handling this journey of unemployment?

Another way of looking at this journey is that it is giving us insight that we would not have if we hadn't gone through it. Studies say that (if you're in my generation) our children are going to have six to eight different jobs or career changes before they are 36. Things are different than they were for our parents; the wheels of progress and change aren't slowing down.

So, when our children say, "you don't understand, I've just lost my job." We can now say we've been there, and tell them, "You have value, and you are currently looking at several opportunities. The question you need to ask yourself is, what do you have to offer, and who needs your help?"

Secret # 4. Say you are "trying to see who **can use your *help.***" Just to recap, when someone asks you, "Have you found a job yet?" That's when you give them your 30-Second commercial, then tell them you are currently looking at several opportunities, and you are trying to see *who could use your "HELP."* You see, when you offer something rather than ask for something, you get a completely different response.

It's about who can I help. You are the answer to someone's problem, and that makes you worth hiring.

The phrase 'how can I help' is a powerful one. What you are conveying is that you have resources that can help, and everyone likes to have a burden lifted. Perhaps you haven't completed your education or gathered a great deal of experience, but you still have resources. You can show up on time, pay attention, and work hard. That is just what some employer is looking for right now. There is nothing wrong with starting right where you are.

Secret #5:
- *Who does what you do?*
- *80% of the jobs are not gotten through postings.*

If it seems like you are applying, applying, and applying but not hearing anything back, it's because most of those jobs have already been filled. Managers, supervisors, directors, the people who do the actual hiring know well in advance when positions are going to be coming available. They are aware of who is going to be promoted, transferred, or is retiring, and they often have someone in mind for the position when it comes open. Federal regulations mandate that 2 weeks before someone leaves, that position has to be posted. Now, poor Human Resources is posting a position and getting 100-500 applications and resumes in for a position that the Hiring authority has perhaps known about for months. I once heard someone say, "That is not fair." I reminded them "Fair" is where we take pigs. Folks, this is just information.

This means that if you are only applying for Posted Jobs, then you are spending 100% of your time on something that is only effective 20% of the time. It's no wonder that it's a slow and frustrating process.

One student told me that they were treating their job search like a full-time job. Okay, that's not a bad way to approach it, but the student was spending 8 hours a day on job search engines and getting no response. I am not saying that you shouldn't utilize the internet in your job search. We will go into detail on how to navigate indeed.com and other job search engines. Just remember that this should not be your primary focus, and that if you are going to use the internet, there are keys to making it more effective.

1. **Apply.** You and 500 people all just did the same thing, right? So then:
2. **Write a cover letter to the hiring authority.** This step will take little research and maybe even some clever sleuthing. The hiring person is not necessarily, or even usually, the human resource department. You will need to identify who in reality will be making the hiring decision. Once you have done this, finding an email/address is usually not that difficult.
3. **Face to face.** Let's face it, people hire people. So how do you get in front of the hiring authority without an invitation? I will go into detail on how to do this in later chapters, but it is as easy as just introducing yourself. I will give you a secret here: NEVER SAY, the "J" word...JOB. This is what I mean, as soon as you say you are looking for a job, people respond negatively because you want something. They will either say one of three things, 1) we are not hiring, 2) apply online, or 3) I don't know of anything. That is why I teach instead of saying you are looking for a JOB, you say, you are looking for **INFORMATION**. People are much more responsive to people needing information rather than needing a job. I had one gentleman run into the hiring authority in Walmart and simply introduce himself and mentioned that he used to work in logistics and was impressed with how well things were organized at the store. He didn't say he was looking for a job. However, he said he would love to get some information about what the needs were in the warehouse. He also conveyed he had worked for 15 years at a Distribution Center and was a Quality Control Manager. By the way, he was implementing Secret #2: The 30-Second Commercial. He walked away with an appointment for an interview.

Networking is the key to finding a job. I want to make sure you know what to say before you get in front of that person.

Chapter Two Key Points:

The Five Secrets:

1. Never say, "I am unemployed"
2. Know Your 30-second commercial (Your Elevator Speech)
3. People want people that other people want... so let them know that you are currently looking at several opportunities!
4. You are the answer to someone's problem... "I am looking to see who could use my HELP"
5. Find out who does what you do... and remember that 80% of the jobs are not gotten through postings.

Chapter Three

Barriers & Blunders

STOP SAYING THE WRONG THINGS

The *Secrets of Landing The Job* is part of a compilation of information that my students learn in my professional development class *Overcoming Job Seeking Barriers and Blunders*. I want you to take a moment and ponder, 'what if you not only took in this information but actually applied it, used it to create change?' Would it **transform** your life? It would certainly make an impact on your job search! I've seen the results myself and have 1000s of success stories from former students who are now gainfully employed.

Yet, even though we know the right thing to do and believe that it will work, many of us still choose not to apply good information. That's crazy talk, right? Why would anyone have the answer and still refuse to solve the problem? You'd be surprised.

Remember the story about losing weight. Believe me, I am an expert at losing weight. I know how to eat right. I know what to do. I understand the purpose and proper use of a treadmill. But when I continue to sit on the couch eating the Twinkie and use my treadmill as a clothes hanger, I will NEVER get the results I want. INFORMATION with APPLICATION leads to TRANSFORMATION! We have to actually apply the information that we know.

If I do, in fact, want results, all I have to do is apply what I know. In other words, I have to let my knowledge guide my decisions, and thus, my actions will produce the corresponding and longed for results. Healthy eating and exercise will put me in the swimsuit I want to wear this summer. If I do anything else, I'm wearing the long T-shirt and dealing with odd tan lines. It's my choice.

The information I am sharing with you in the book will give you the power (knowledge) to make **life-changing decisions**. It will **transform** how people see you because it will transform how you see YOURSELF.

No more 'shape of an L' on your forehead, loser sign for you!

You understand that you have "a very particular set of skills. Skills you have acquired over your career," which make you valuable… and that changes things.

Remember we said that the answer to the question *'So what do you do'* is never *'I am unemployed'*? The problem with most people who are looking for a job is they say the WRONG things and fail to present themselves as value-added. Employers too often hear the WRONG responses to the question, "Tell me about yourself?" People say:

- I am currently unemployed. **X-WRONG**
- I'm not doing anything right now. **X-WRONG**
- I got laid off. **X-WRONG**
- I'm looking for a job. **X-WRONG**

These are all just different ways of saying the wrong thing! First, remember whether you are employed or not, you still have the same experience, education, and value! Second, none of these statements relate your experience, education, or value to the person who is **obviously** interested in you.

Honestly, when I hear someone answer like this, I hold up my finger to my forehead, forming the letter "L." As if to say, "Lost Opportunity" or "Loser."

NOOOOOO, that is not who you are or what you want! Remember that unemployed is your current circumstance, it is NOT who you are! Please understand how important this concept is to your success.

I understand that is a natural response to tell someone your current circumstance, but unless they specifically ask you where you are working, it doesn't matter. Stick to telling them why they should be interested in having you as part of their team. The truth of the matter is they need you to be available so that you can work for them!

We communicate in many different ways, whether it is through words or body language. When a potential employer inquires about you, they are looking for how you can help them be successful. It is never good to start with a perceived negative, such as *I am unemployed*. People, no one is going to hire someone who is down or depressed. They are not going to hire you because You Need a Job. They are going to hire you because **they need you**! They need your experience, your education, and your energy, and they've asked you to tell them about THOSE things.

Remember ***Negativity is natural, but Positivity is Powerful!***

Your life is about to change.

Let's get into more detail about the **5 Secrets of Landing The Job** and how to avoid the typical Barriers & Blunders.

Secret #1: **Never say, "I am unemployed looking for a Job."**

I know what you are thinking. It's like beating a dead horse, but you only get one chance to make a first impression. This is also the greatest barrier and blunder for most people in their job search and the most difficult habit to break.

Saying you're unemployed does NOT give anyone (including yourself) useful information. It does not tell them who you are or what you are capable of, all it does is tell people your current circumstances.

Tip: Do not ***define yourself*** by your circumstances.

Often, I hear people say I just need a job, I'll do anything. Well, first of all, there aren't many employers looking to hire someone to just do anything. Employers are looking to hire people who meet specific needs. They want to hire someone who can do what they need to be done.

Quite frankly, it's a simple equation:

$$A\ Problem + A\ Solution = A\ Job$$

They are looking for the solution to their particular problem. That's what you are to them; an answer to a problem. Perhaps you are a graphic designer, and the local sign company is growing and can't keep up with the work. You would be the answer to their particular problem. Maybe the parks and recreation department is putting in a new sports facility, and you have some experience running small equipment. They have a need or a problem, and you are the answer they are looking for, but they won't know that until you communicate it to them.

Also, I don't care what you say, you won't do just ANYTHING, or at least, you won't do it for very long. Besides, how do you even know that you would be qualified to do just any old thing?

It's been said that anything worth doing is worth doing right and searching for employment certainly falls under this category. It is best to take the time and make the effort to find a job that fits you and that you are qualified for. Remember, the employer is looking for someone who can solve their problem, and if you aren't qualified to do so, then you can't solve their problem.

Tip: You are far more likely to stay and be successful if you invest in doing the job search the right way.

Secret #2: Learn your "30-Second Commercial."

Several years ago, someone came up with the idea that every company, organization, institution, sports league, and civic group needed a well-defined Mission Statement. This statement was similar to a slogan but with a little more clarity so that the public would know instantly who they were. It was *short, concise, and easy for people to understand.* In short, the company mission statement communicated who the company was or their identity!

The idea of the *30-Second Commercial* or *Elevator Speech* works in much the same manner. Most of us abhor public speaking, in fact, one report states that 74% of the population suffers from speech anxiety. What does this mean? It means that we often struggle to communicate under pressure. Yet, how will people know our worth if we can't communicate it? This is precisely the reason that we should develop a rehearsed presentation specifically to reply to questions like 'What do you do?' or 'tell me about yourself.'

Put together a quick synopsis of your education and experience that highlights your value to a potential employer... and then practice it. Practice your speech in front of a mirror, practice it in your car, while your jogging, tell it to your spouse, your children, and even your pet. Your pet should want to hire you!

In your 30-Second Commercial, communicate what you know, what you have done, and where you have worked instead of just saying, "I am unemployed."

Remember that stating I am unemployed communicates nothing except negativity.

Tip: *The best predictor of the future is the past.*

Keeping this in mind, let's look over a couple of examples of effective 30-Second Commercials:

Example #1:

"I have 20 years of experience in manufacturing. I have worked in production, shipping and receiving, and quality assurance. I worked for NACCO and ASMO. One of the things I am most proud of is while at NACCO, I received recognition for a suggestion I made that simplified our packaging system and saved the company quite a bit of money."

By saying where you worked and what you did, it allows people to know what it is you are capable of.

Example #2:

"I served in the Marines for 7 years. I served several tours during Desert Storm and then in Afghanistan. After my enlistment in the Military, I received my Master's in Human Resources, with a Bachelor's degree in Business Administration. I have a passion for helping organizations find good people. I have also been a soccer coach for the past 5 years and enjoy developing our young people."

Example #3:

"I was the team leader and project manager for a regional software company called Knowledgeware. One of my strengths was keeping the team on track to reach their goals while managing a 2.3 million-dollar budget. I was also responsible for quality control and final inspection of our products as well as client relations."

Example #4:

"I work with the future. For the past 10 years, I've had the opportunity to educate middle school students as a social science teacher. I also served as a coach for various sports and mentored more students than I can count. I love being a part of a team and helping students find confidence and develop their own voice."

These are just a few examples, and obviously, yours should be tailored to your experience and education as well as your own voice. These are prepared and rehearsed, but they should also be natural and sound like you.

It is also perfectly acceptable to include what you are currently looking for in regard to employment. If you were an educator but are looking to transition into public relations, mention that in your short elevator speech and include why you think the skill set is transferrable.

"After working with hundreds of pubescent teenagers for the last ten years, I think that I can handle pretty much any type of crowd."

Remember, we want to share our experience and skills to create an interest in the listener to learn more about us. In essence, the 30-Second Commercial is our business card, and it lets people know who we are and what we can do for them.

This brings us to my favorite secret. This is something I hope you start implementing TODAY!

After people ask you 'What do you do?' and you don't respond with 'I am unemployed' but rather let them know what you enjoy and what you are qualified to do, the next question will almost always be, "Where do you work?" Or if they know that you have been looking for employment, they will phrase it, "Have you found a job yet... loser?"

Never let these questions bother you. You know that they're coming, so let's be ready for them. Here is my absolute favorite secret. When people ask if you've found a job yet, here is what you **must** reply:

Secret #3: "I am currently looking at several opportunities."

Folks, I am telling you that this is going to be a game-changer in your job search. The reality is, "people want people that other people want!" In the early 80s, everyone had to have a Cabbage Patch doll. Honestly, there wasn't anything particularly special about these dolls, but they were a must-have Christmas present. The same thing happened when Michael Jordan became the face of Nike, and suddenly, Reebok was yesterday's news.

The truth is that in your job search, you are legitimately exploring as many opportunities as you can find. This is crucial for not only them to understand but for you as well. The process of searching for employment isn't you randomly running from place to place searching for the gatekeeper. It is equally important for you to evaluate your prospective employer to see if they are a worthy match for your talent.

The next time someone asks, "Have you found a job yet?" just smile and say. "Actually, *I am currently looking at several opportunities.*" Then share your 30-Second commercial so they know who you are and what you have done.

Example: "You know, I have had the privilege of working in Higher Education for the past 20 years at places like Gardner-Webb University, Cleveland Community College, and Pitt Community College in workforce Development."

Remember, it is true that you are looking at several opportunities. What they don't need to know is where you are in that process. The truth is you are looking and applying... they don't need to know if those opportunities have or haven't called you back yet. If they ask you which opportunities you are looking into, don't be afraid to let them know. What are they going to do, call those organizations and ask where you are in the hiring process? Of course not, but knowing that you are exploring options will create a sense of urgency for prospective employers to make a hiring decision.

After saying your 30-second commercial and that you currently looking at several opportunities;

NOW YOU SAY:

Secret #4: "I am trying to see who can use my HELP."

Remember that you are there to be the **answer** or **solution** to someone's problem. You are not there for **charity.** You increase the value or productivity of the employer's business, and thus, you are there to *help* them!

"Help" is the key word in your job search. What you are searching for is a place that can benefit from you being there; who can use your help. I know that you may have that sinking, desperate *I just need a job* feeling, but let's remember to not panic because you are not broken, nor have you lost your value.

You may feel like you need help, like you have failed, like you have lost your worth, but sometimes, our emotions are just a product of our poor thinking. Sure, you are currently unemployed, but everyone is employable, everyone has something to offer. When you stop looking for help and begin to look for somewhere to be helpful, everything is going to change.

First, when we say, "I'm looking for a job," people are prone to be a bit defensive. They don't know exactly what you bring to the table or how you could help them solve their problems, and they are usually a bit reticent to take the risk of hiring you without knowing what they will get in return. In other words, you've asked them to help you solve your problem. This is not something most employers are interested in doing.

Now, when you say, "I am trying to see who could use my help," then you are more accurately representing your intentions. You need a job, but what you truly desire is to find a place where what you are good at is valued and appreciated. You want to find somewhere that they will pay you to invest yourself.

Tip: I'm looking for someone who can use my help implies that you are offering something versus asking for something.

This mindset and approach is a far more accurate depiction of your goal. You aren't going empty-handed to an employer looking for undeserved charity. You are offering your education, experience, and energy to their organization for their benefit in return for equitable compensation. You are worth them offering you a job **because** of who you are and what you bring to the table.

When you say, "I'm looking for a job. Are you hiring?" you can usually count on a negative response, such as:

- I'm sorry, we are not hiring.
- I don't know of anyone hiring.
- Come back next week.
- You need to go online and apply.

(I know if you hear "apply online" one more time, you are going to scream!)

So it is important to keep in mind that people are more open when we offer them something (How can I help your business) than when we request something from them (I need a job).

Remember, it is often how we say something that makes the real difference!

Secret #5 80% of the jobs out there are NOT gotten through answering a posting

What? What about Monster, Indeed, and the Employment Security Commission? So, let me pull back the veil and explain how this actually works. Job postings are done by a company's human resource department. Most of the time, they are one or two steps removed from the position that they are posting and are not actually the people that will make the final hiring decisions.

When you got your last job, who hired you? This is a question that I ask pretty much everyone that I work with, and almost without exception, no one answers 'HR.' The person that hired them was the manager, supervisor, director, or owner, and then they were sent to HR to do the paperwork. People in positions of authority know what jobs are open, what jobs are coming open, and they do the hiring for these jobs.

Why? These are the people who know who going to be let go, who is going to be promoted, and who is going to be transferred long before HR ever gets wind of it. They also understand the growth potential and challenges their company is facing and what opportunities are on the horizon. Therefore, they know what positions are going to be needed way before HR ever has the opportunity to post them. In fact, studies show that they often know three to four months out, or further, what positions will need to be filled, and they are already looking for the right people to fill them.

Federal regulations mandate that 2 weeks before a person leaves, the position needs to be posted for Equal Opportunity. Once that position is posted, you might have 100 to 500 applications and resumes coming in for that one position, and keep in mind, the person with the hiring authority has usually been 'looking' for someone to meet the need for quite a while.

In essence, when you rely solely on job postings, you are spending 100% of your time on 20% of the jobs. Were you aware of this fact? It's no wonder you are so frustrated. There is nothing wrong with applying for jobs that are posted, but putting all of your eggs in that basket is not an effective way to search for the right job. So the question you want to ask yourself is, 'who knows about the positions coming up?' Because your real goal is to get to them before the job even gets posted.

I know you know everything that we just went over, but when you are in the middle of being 'unemployed,' it is easy to forget important things like how we were hired or promoted at our last job. Also, in the midst of this journey, we can become overwhelmed, that is why I want to remind you how positions are created.

How do jobs become available?
- People leaving
- Company expansions
- Promotion
- Restructuring
- New Management
- Mergers and Acquisitions
- Economy Boom
- Retirement/Death

Let's face it, jobs can sometimes get scarce, but there is always a market for good workers. More importantly, the job market is constantly changing, and jobs are constantly being made available, even in down markets. You just have to know where to look.

We need to be talking to the people who know about these things way before they are posted. I teach NEVER SAY you are looking for a job. Instead, say you are just looking for **INFORMATION**. You can get in front of any hiring authority if the purpose is to get information from an expert in the field. As we move along, we will address this idea in greater detail. However, you already know a few key secrets that will help you accomplish this task:

Secret #3

"I am currently looking at several opportunities, but before making a decision, I wanted to talk to an expert in the field to understand what the needs are in the industry."

Your goal now is to learn how to get in front of the hiring authority to get access to the 80% of the jobs that aren't posted. The key to unlocking this opportunity is certainly not stating that *'you are unemployed.'*

You are also going to learn how to maximize your chances with that 20% of jobs that are posted. The good news is you've already taken the first step and applied online. We will discuss the next 2 vital steps soon.

Now that you know 80% of the jobs are not posted, you need to ask yourself a very important question:

"Who does or needs what I do?"

Chapter Three Key Points:

Barriers and Blunders

1. Stop saying the wrong thing. Negativity is Natural, but Positivity is Powerful.
2. Do not **define yourself** by your circumstances.
3. "I'm looking for someone who can use my help" implies that you are offering something versus asking for something.
4. Remember: 80% of the jobs out there are NOT gotten through answering a posting.
5. Say you are looking for INFORMATION, this will get you in front of the right people.

Chapter Four

The Cover Letter: Make The Proper (Effective) First Impression

---
"A SOLUTION TO A PROBLEM."

General Electric exists to produce electricity, Wachovia's purpose is banking, John Hopkins provides Healthcare, and the University of Georgia excels in education as well as football, and they all do their jobs with excellence. They are not, however, in the 'hiring' business. Yes, hiring employees is a necessary *evil* for them to meet their stated objectives, but it is not their purpose. And yet, we say, "I sent my application in for a position, why hasn't anyone contacted me?"

Perhaps it is because they are BUSY doing their jobs. It is imperative that we keep in mind that they aren't interested in hiring you to solve *your* problem. They honestly do not care that you are currently unemployed and need a job. Remember, their purpose is producing *electricity* or *winning* national titles, not hiring you.

So when a company or organization looks at you, it is entirely for selfish reasons. They want to know if you can solve **their** problem, fill **their** need, make **them** better. If the answer is yes, then you are hired; cue the music put on your dancing shoes, it's nothing but champagne and caviar from now on. If the answer is no, then you may get the perfunctory *Dear John (Applicant)* letter saying thanks, but no thanks, please move along.

Your **Value**, and remember that everyone has **Value**, is the fact that to someone, you are the answer that they are looking for. Thus, you hold the key to their success. Yes, you may be a small part of a much larger puzzle, but a puzzle is only good if you have *all* the pieces.

If you understand what a company does, then you can begin to ask yourself how you might be an asset to that organization. What do they need? What problem can you solve that allows them to make money or save money to reach their goal? Because that is the **Only** reason for them to hire you.

So when you are introducing yourself to a potential employer, keep in mind two important things: (Nothing else matters).

What do they do, and why do they need you to get it done?

There are several steps to this *Employment Dance,* and it's good to not only know them but to be good at them. Assuming that you have identified an organization with a need that you are confident that you can meet, then it is time to 'introduce' yourself. The first formal means of introduction comes in the form of the *Cover Letter*.

A cover letter is defined as *"a letter sent with and explaining the contents of another document."* This may seem a bit silly, and in some ways, it may be, but it is also one more way for you to make a good impression. So if it has to be done, then we might as well do it well.

So now, let's imagine ourselves as a potential employer. We have a problem, and we need someone to join our team that can fix it. To make this happen, we have to **stop** our daily routine and turn our attention to the hiring process. We are busy, and perhaps more importantly, we don't like this part of our job. We approach it with the same zeal and expectation as our 8th-grade summer reading assignments, squeezing it in between our last morning meeting and lunch. We grudgingly open the folder containing the stack of applicant packages and come across this gem of a cover letter.

JOHN ROGERS
123 Main Street
Shelby, NC 28150
(704) 555-5555
RogersJohn@yahoo.com

March 26, 2006

Timothy T. Mellon
Director of College Recruiting
Midwest Mercantile Company
4500 Randolph Drive
Chicago, IL 60601

Dear Mr. Mellon:

While researching companies, I read your company's description in NACE's Job Choices in Business and would like to inquire about employment opportunities in your management training program. I want to work in retail management and would like to relocate to the Chicago area after graduation.

I will receive my Bachelor of Science Degree this May. My interest in business started in Junior Achievement while in high school and developed further through a variety of sales and retail positions during college. My internship with a large department store convinced me to pursue a career in retail. When I researched the top retailers in Chicago, Midwest Mercantile emerged as having a strong market position, an excellent training program, and a reputation for excellent customer service. In short, you provide the kind of professional retail environment I seek.

My education and experience match the qualifications you seek in your management trainees, but they don't tell the whole story. I know from customer and supervisor feedback that I have the interpersonal skills and motivation needed to build a successful career in retail management. And my relatively extensive experience gives me confidence in my career direction and in my abilities to perform competently.

My credentials are enclosed for your review. I realize your schedule is hectic, but I would greatly appreciate the chance to discuss employment possibilities with you. Feel free to contact me at (704) 555-5555 or by e-mail at Rogers.John@yahoo.com. Thank you very much for considering my request. I look forward to speaking with you.

Sincerely,

(Handwritten signature)

John Rogers

What did you notice about this cover letter? If you answered nothing, then not only are you honest, but you are also correct. Much like our 8th grade selves, we still abhor mandatory reading, and much like our 8th grade reading list, the material is about as exciting as watching paint dry. Furthermore, unlike our 8th grade selves, we actually do have more 'important' things to do than wade our way through 500 personnel essays about people we don't know when all we really care about is, "Can they help us?"

We look at the name, and that is it. We don't READ. We look and see a lot of WORDS, but *nothing stands out* because, again, we don't read. It doesn't matter how heartfelt, inspiring, or life-changing your letter may actually be because employers are not *actually* reading it.

Tell the truth; when you saw it was just an example of a cover letter, you turned the page. You DIDN'T read it. The key to your future may have been in that letter, but you would have missed it because it was buried under so much junk.

Folks, let me tell you something, people spend 15-30 seconds reviewing most documents. They are looking for what you can do for them, nothing more! This may seem a bit callous, but it's no different than when you are looking for an item in one of those large home improvement box stores. You're not interested in someone telling you how they came about being employed there, even if it is a good story. You just want to know where to find the part for your ice maker, and if the clueless employee can't answer that question, then what good are they to you?

Now let's look at an example of a more effective cover letter, one that doesn't read like *Of Mice and Men*.

ROGER SMITH II, EIT

116 Smith Circle, Dallas NC 28034, (704)576-1234, roger24@yahoo.com

---

February 5, 2010

Ms. Southerland,

I am writing to let you know about my interest in the **Special Project Engineer** position currently available in Shelby, NC. After reviewing the scope of responsibilities, I feel I have all the necessary credentials and would be the perfect candidate for this position.

The enclosed resume reflects a match between my credentials and your requirements for this engineering position. A qualification summary follows:

JOB REQUIREMENTS	PERSONAL QUALIFICATIONS
Bachelor's Degree in Mechanical Engineering	• Bachelor of Science in Mechanical Engineering Technology, UNC Charlotte, ABET Accredited
Be familiar with the cad system	• Over ten (12) years' experience with AutoCAD 2D & 3D. Working knowledge of various other CAD and CAE (Computer Aided Engineering) software.
Self-motivated and ability to work with others	• Very self-motivated, enjoy working in a team environment. Continuously in a "thinking out of the box" situations. Fast-paced, multi-tasking environment while keeping a sense of urgency to complete job responsibilities.
Plans, organizes product design, testing, scheduling, and problem-solving	• Involved with progressive engineering for over five (5) years, including but not limited to product design and engineering.

I feel certain with my engineering experience, and my ability to communicate with team members will be of immediate value. Should you agree, after reviewing my resume, I would welcome a personal meeting to further discuss your needs and my abilities to meet them.

Best regards,

Roger Smith II, EIT

When looking at this cover letter, what is the first thing you notice?

The name: **'Roger Smith II'** It is BIG and BOLD.

What does he want? **'Special Projects Engineer'** How do we know? It is clearly highlighted and easy to pick out of the text.

Where do our eyes go next? **'Personal Qualifications'** Here, Mr. Smith has listed his qualifications in clear bullet points as they relate to the job requirements. In other words, he is stating succinctly how he can solve Mr. Southerland's problem.

The great thing is you can RELAX, this really awesome cover letter is on my website, and you are more than welcome to download it and make it your own. YEAH!!!!

Better news, it is in a Word document so you can just save it to your desktop, or flash drive, and then change the name and information. It's in Word document rather than a Word template because templates are evil mischievous creatures that refuse to be tamed and end up driving good people to do things that they regret later. Word docs are easy, so be excited!

Chapter Four Key Points:

First Impressions: The Cover Letter

1. Potential employers: What do they do, and why do they need you to get it done?
2. Can you help them? Remember, you aren't just looking for a job, you are looking for the right fit.
3. A Cover Letter isn't really a letter... it's a highlight, so keep it simple and easy.

Chapter Five

The Dynamic Resume: Getting the Interview

"COME ON IN"

As you have probably already figured out, almost every employer now has an 'online application' process that they are extremely proud of, and that rarely works properly. So then the question you may be wondering is, 'Why do we even have to have a resume?'

There are 3 good reasons why you Want and Need a resume:

1. A well-developed resume will be a lifesaver when you are filling out those long detailed online applications. Having your information in front of you will help you be accurate and impactful.
2. You shouldn't rely on your 'application' to communicate who you are to an employer. When you go into an interview and meet that manager, do you really think that they are going to look at that 10 – 15 page application with your birth date, social security number, and where you went to High School. "NOOOOOO." You **want** that one-page piece of paper that plainly highlights your qualifications
Example:
    a. Increased sales
    b. Decreased wastes
    c. Implemented
    d. Facilitated

These are things that are not on your application, but your resume helps a hiring manager to quickly recognize your capabilities.
3. Your resume helps you formulate what verbiage you want to use when putting your 30-second commercial together. Think of it as **Branding** yourself, and the Resume is the device that you use to frame 'everything' else.

So, if we liken the Cover Letter to ringing the proverbial doorbell, then the resume is akin to speaking with someone on their doorstep. Essentially, what has transpired is that the employer has peered through the small peephole and determined that you warrant a closer look, so they open the door. This is still not a face to face encounter but rather another opportunity for you to wow them with your written communication skills in the form of your resume.

Yet, not all resumes are created equal, and thus, we must be careful to not blow this opportunity by putting forth a jumbled mess of information rather than clearly articulating why we should be granted an interview. As Joe Friday was so fond of saying, "Just the facts ma'am," should be our mantra.

The same lessons that we learned regarding the cover letter apply to the development of our dynamic resume. Therefore, keep in mind that people don't read, they skim in search of *key* information that specifically answers the questions that *they* are interested in. More to the point, how do you meet their needs?

Let's take a look at some resumes.

NAME
9988 Rockridge Drive
Oakland CA 94609
(510) 987-6543
JIMDOE@YAHOO.COM

OBJECTIVE

A position as MACHINIST.

HIGHLIGHTS

- Ten years' experience as Machinist.
- Journeyman machinist, California licensed.
- Proven ability to independently handle specialized projects at remote worksites.
- Extremely broad experience with all kinds of machine tools and materials.
- Responsible, dependable, punctual; take pride in my work.

RELEVANT SKILLS & EXPERIENCE

GENERAL MACHINING

- Set up and operated: -lathes   -mills   -precision grinders   -turret lathes   -horizontal and vertical boring mills   -planers   -slotters   -shapers   -NC machines
- Used fixtures such as   -dividing heads   -indexing heads   -vises   -knees   -angle plates   -taper attachments   -rotary tables   -steady and follow rests
- Performed precision measurement and layout using such instruments as:
    - -micrometers: inside, outside, pitch
    - -gauges: depth, surface, height, Mueller, ring, plug
    - -calipers: dial, vernier   -scales: 6" through 72"
    - -precision squares and protractors   -dial indicators
- Worked with documents: -blueprints   -sketches   -design memos   -technical requirements   -military standards   -Machinery Handbook

MATERIALS EXPERIENCE

- Machined a broad range of materials including: -mild steel -HY-80 -high carbon steel -stainless steel -monel -brass -nickel aluminum bronze -stellite -cobalt -titanium -aluminum -Delren -Teflon

SPECIAL PROJECT

- As lead machinist, assigned to work independently on 90-day submarine overhaul projects at remote sites:
    - -Planned and shipped all necessary tools to the job site.
    - -Acted as machinist-liaison, coordinating machining with the work of other trades.
    - -Designed and manufactured test equipment and special tooling needed for overhaul.
    - -Accomplished a variety of special setups with limited machine tools.

WORK HISTORY

1993-94	*Student*	Solano Community College, Suisun CA – career exploration
	Part-time sales	(concurrent with school)
1992-92	*Machinist*	PUGET SOUND NAVAL SHIPYARD, Bremerton WA
1983-92	*Machinist*	PUGET SOUND NAVAL SHIPYARD, Vallejo CA

EDUCATION

Four-year **Machinist Apprenticeship:** Mare Island Naval Shipyard, 1983-87
Solano Community College, Suisun CA, 1979
Major: Ship Building/Machine Tool Technology

What is the applicant's stated objective? **'A position as a Machinist.'**

Did we have to labor through some long paragraph? No! It wasn't a soliloquy that read, "I want to work for a challenging organization that will utilize my education as well as my experience working with stuff."

Remember that they are simply looking for a person to solve their problem, and for them, it's the fact that they need a machinist. It's what they advertised for, and it is what the applicant does. So, if the employer is rifling through the resumes like an 8th grader skimming the Cliff Notes, it's important for Joe Applicant to state his facts in a way that gets them noticed, brief and highlighted!

Let's face it, this is not rocket science. Joe Applicant does what they need, it's a match, nothing more needs to be said.

After the name and objective (job desired), you will find Joe's summary of his experience. These are listed in short bullet points under Highlights:

- Ten years' experience as a Machinist.
- Journeyman machinist, California licensed.
- Proven ability to independently handle specialized projects at remote worksites.
- Extremely broad experience with all kinds of machine tools and materials.
- Responsible, dependable, punctual; take pride in my work.

You don't have to use the heading of Highlights; a number of things could work, such as Work Summary, Experience, Past Performance. What matters is that they are concise and easy to find. If they are done properly, like Joe's here, then the employer already knows that he can do the job. He's obviously done it before or something similar for someone else. This section truly is the Cliff Notes version of the information that follows.

Next, you have a section listing the applicant's Relevant Skills & Experience. This area breaks down the things that you have done and supports what you listed in the Highlights section in a more defined way.

My friends, this is not a Chronological Resume. Those are what one might refer to as old school, antiquated, not hip. The Chronological Resume says this is where I worked, and this is what I did over and over again. Sure, the employer may be able to extrapolate the necessary information out of this dull procession of facts, but it is not a very effective way to communicate your skills. The Chronological Resume depends on the employer taking their time and reading for comprehension, which we've already established doesn't usually happen. If you want the interview, which is the purpose of the resume in the first place, you have to make your impact quick before they shut the door and leave you standing on the front porch.

That's why we are focusing on the Functional Resume. It allows us to *reveal* to the employer why we are worth investing the time and energy necessary for an interview in a way that is quick and easy for them. Thus, we've already solved one problem for them... we've made the hiring process easier. That makes us problem solvers in their eyes, and after all, isn't that what they are looking for?

Now, before you ask, "does that mean I have to have a different resume for different jobs?" The answer is, "NO." Let's take a look at another Functional resume, and I will show you what I mean.

MIRIAM "Beth" Black

588 EAST MARION ST ◆ SHELBY, NC ◆ (704-482-1234)

bethblack@yahoo.com

OBJECTIVE

CUSTOMER SERVICE/MANAGEMENT

SUMMARY OF QUALIFICATIONS

- 11 Years of Customer Service Experience
- 5 years of Customer Service Management
- Problem-solving & Conflict Management Skills
- Cross-trained new hire cashiers
- Cross-trained 5 members of Management
- Dependable employee, team player, and fast learner
- Knowledgeable in customer service environment
- Committed and dependable

SKILLS & ACCOMPLISHMENTS

Customer Service
- Possess strong communication and organizational skills.
- Linked customers with informational resources as value-added service.
- Leveraged position with customers, offering an impressive record for service and reliability.
- Responsible for the accuracy of information about products, inventory control, and scheduling.
- Met challenges head on; work well in stressful situations and in a fast-paced setting.

Leadership
- Managed various areas of Department Store, built modular, worked effectively with employees and customers
- Strong Problem-Solving Skills and Conflict Management Skills
- *Ten year Safety Award, Five star Cashier Award*
- Mastered the Art Of Challenging Customers.

Organization Skills
- Maintained orderly departments and work schedules of cashiers.
- Managed customer support representatives in various departments.
- Cross-trained employee's in various departments of Super Center Department Store.

WORK EXPERIENCE

1998-2010	*Customer Service Manager*	**Wal-Mart Supercenter**, Gastonia, NC
1996-1997	*Sander/Sprayer*	**Rex Furniture Company**, Rex, GA
1995-1996	*Material Handler/Machine Operator*	**Polygram Inc.**, Grover, NC
1992-1994	*Cosmetologists*	**York Hair Salon**, Gastonia, NC

EDUCATION

SHELBY HIGH SCHOOL, Shelby, NC
Diploma 1989

CLEVELAND COMMUNITY COLLEGE, Shelby, NC
Success: Landing My Next Job

Again, with our employer hat on, we already know who she is and what she wants to do because Beth stated it clearly and boldly at the top of the page with no fluff. She desires a position in customer service or management. Assuming that our company or organization has a problem in one of these areas, then we know that she might fit the bill, so we skim over her Highlights.

Boom! There it is, 11 years of customer experience and 5 years in management. Is she qualified to do the job? According to this, she is, and we didn't have to waste time digging for it. It was right there in the bullet points under Qualifications.

Need more information to support Beth's qualifications? Like what type of customer service was she primarily responsible for, or in what capacity did she serve as a leader? To find the answers to these questions, all we have to do is check out her Skills and Accomplishment section.

Here we find categories such as:

- Customer Service
- Leadership
- Organizational Skills

What if you were a Machine Operator with Supervisory experience? Then your categories might read:

- Manufacturing
- Machine Operator
- Leadership

What if you were an Office Administrator? You might list your categories like this:

- Office Administration
- Customer Service
- Organizational Skills

The bottom line is that you want to put forth the areas that demonstrate your ability to perform the requirements for the position you desire. You want them to see your value; this is your opportunity to express that value, to make yourself marketable.

One of my students shared a concern with me that went something like this. 'I have been working since I was 16 years old, and so I have over 35 years of work experience. However, I am worried they are going to try and do the math and think I am too old?'

She had a good point. If you have worked for 27, 35, or even 40 years, then it's probably not a good idea that you put an emphasis on those numbers... in fact, we will go so far as to say you never emphasis those numbers. It's like going on a date, we don't want to hide information because it's all going to come out eventually, but there are things to lead with and things to share later. Often, the key to success is knowing when and what to share.

So how would you describe your work experience in this situation? 20+ years will sufficiently convey your experience without providing too much detail in the resume. Here is the thing, your work experience may state that you've worked from 1979-2009, which quick math tells us that's a 30-year span, but remember, they aren't reading paragraphs. Most aren't even reading the entire bullet point. They are skimming at most, and they surely aren't taking the time to do the math. Truthfully, for most positions, age is not important, and for all positions, age is of far less interest than whether or not you are qualified. So let's lead with your qualifications, and we will dicker over your possible gray hair later. This goes for any other distraction you may feel might hinder your opportunity... lead with your best.

A Functional resume is effective because it allows you to demonstrate your Skills and Abilities to a prospective employer rather than focusing on how long you've worked! Remember that the goal is to show that you can solve their problem because you've successfully done so for others in the past. You get results, which is the impression that the resume should leave with anyone who reads it.

Elephant in the Room: There are some tricky issues that often must be addressed during our job search, such as the 'age' issue that was mentioned earlier. Things like gaps in employment while you went back to school or even periods of incarceration. There are ways to handle these **professionally** while putting your best self forward on your resume.

Let's identify the proper verbiage that will allow you to stand out to an employer! Take a moment and look over Oliver's resume:

Oliver W. Homestead

3838 N. Enfelt Ave.　　　　　　Portland, OR 97217　　　　　　(503) 282-2828

OBJECTIVE
Position as a Machinist

HIGHLIGHTS OF QUALIFICATIONS
- Creative, independent machinist/millwright with strong mechanical aptitude.
- Fifteen years of experience in various aspects of machine repair and operation.
- Ability to work independently as well as a team player.
- Adept at "seeing" a problem and finding a solution.

RELEVANT EXPERIENCE
- Supervised and trained employees on the use of various equipment.
- Set up work schedules for machinists according to job priorities and machine size.
- Operated largest and newest CNC Super Profile Multi-Spindle Milling Machines.
- Troubleshot, repaired, and maintained heavy mill equipment.
- Developed hands-on knowledge of a variety of hand and power tools.
- Learned to skillfully read blueprints and schematics.
- Set up and operated a variety of machinery.
- Received three cash awards for projection enhancement suggestions.
- Received ACE Award for performance and named "Employee of the Month."

EQUIPMENT OPERATED

• Lathes	• Surface Grinders	• Allen Bradley 8600
• Milling Machines	• Key Seaters	• Cincinnati Millacron
• Radial Drill Press	• Cylindrical Grinder	Control
• Horizontal boring Mill	• Fanuc M6	• Mobile Cranes
	• GE Fanuc 15	

WORK HISTORY

CNC MACHINIST, Boeing of Portland　　　　　　1986-present
CNC MACHINIST, Western Iron Works　　　　　　1985-1986
MACHINIST/MILLWRIGHT, Cascade Steel Mill Corporation　　1974-1984

EDUCATION
Mt. Hood Community College – Career/Life Planning

Portland Community College – **Machine Technology**

We know right out of the gate who he is and what he wants because that information is clearly listed on the top of the page, but what can Oliver do? After all, that is the information that will tell us if he is right for the job, isn't it?

When an employer reads over the section of Oliver's resume entitled Equipment Operated, they will come away with a deeper understanding of what Oliver is capable of doing for them. They now know not only that he a machinist, but they also have a detailed list of tools that he has worked with in the past.

In short, the resume conveys to the employer what you can do in the future for them because of what you've already done in the past for someone else, otherwise known as Experience. This is why we need to become familiar with key words, verbiage, that helps your Experience pop out to employers when they 'read' your resume.

Okay, let's get back to examining another resume:

MATERIALS EXPERIENCE
- Machined a broad range of materials including: -mild steel -HY-80 -high carbon steel -stainless steel -monel -brass -nickel aluminum bronze -stellite -cobalt -titanium -aluminum -Delren -Teflon

SPECIAL PROJECT
- As lead machinist, assigned to work independently on 90-day submarine overhaul projects at remote sites:
    - Planned and shipped all necessary tools to the job site.
    - Acted as machinist-liaison, coordinating machining with the work of other trades.
    - Designed and manufactured test equipment and special tooling needed for overhaul.
    - Accomplished a variety of special setups with limited machine tools.

WORK HISTORY

1993-94	Student	Solano Community College, Suisun CA – career exploration
	Part-time sales	(concurrent with school)
1992-92	Machinist	PUGET SOUND NAVAL SHIPYARD, Bremerton WA
1983-92	Machinist	PUGET SOUND NAVAL SHIPYARD, Vallejo CA

EDUCATION

Four-year **Machinist Apprenticeship:** Mare Island Naval Shipyard, 1983-87
Solano Community College, Suisun CA, 1979
Major: Ship Building/Machine Tool Technology

Unemployed: Notice under Work History on the previous page that they are currently listing themselves as a "Student." Listen folks, employers are hesitant to hire someone that is unemployed. I know what you are thinking, "that's not fair... they want me to have an education, but they are going to penalize me for taking the time to get that education?" You are right, it's not fair, but unfortunately, it is often true. However, there are ways to overcome this issue of human nature.

I suggest to the students that attend my professional development classes to become experts at knowing their **brand.** Yes, you may be a student or working on your Career Readiness Certification, Electricians License, what have you, but you are not unemployed. You are working hard, even if it is to just find a job!

So this is what it sounds like when you ask the 'what are you doing now' question to one of my students, "I have 15 years of experience doing this, that, or the other, and I am currently looking at several opportunities. In the meantime, I am taking classes at (insert college name here) to gain a deeper understanding and experience of (insert field of study) while I talk to people to see who could really use my help."

Does that not sound better than "I'm unemployed and can't find a job?" Sure it does, and there are a couple of reasons for it.

First, you don't throw out that word 'unemployed,' which elicits such a negative reaction from people. Perhaps we should take a moment and ask ourselves why they have this reaction so that we can let ourselves off the hook. In our culture, there is a great amount of emphasis placed on one's job and the ability to support ourselves, it makes us good people. So when someone is unemployed, regardless of the reasons why, there is a faulty premise that they are no longer 'good' or that somehow they have lost their value. This is just not true.

Second, you have redirected to 'what' you do, which is far more important than where you do something. Furthermore, you have expressed to them that you are a lifelong learner who is in the process of personal and professional development. These are traits that every employer desires in their workforce.

Also, most of the people I am working with are doing some kind of work on the side while they are unemployed, which means that 'technically,' they are working. They may not be receiving a paycheck, but that doesn't actually define work, and some of the greatest learning experiences come without a paycheck! So if you are working on the side, here is a rule of thumb... can you get a reference?

For instance, if Jim says he is "Self-employed as a Handyman," the employer may want to know what kind of work he has been doing. For Jim, it may be that he has helped put a roof on his friend's house, and remember, even if he did not get paid, it's still a job that he has done, an experience that he can claim, and a reference that he can give!

An employer is not going to ask for a 1099 or a W2. That employer wants to know did you do work for someone and what was that work. If you are doing consulting, childcare, editing, web design, it's all the same. The only stipulation is that it has to be for 'someone' else. You can't be parenting your own children and list childcare experience or cleaning your own home and claiming domestic engineer on your application. Remember, you have to have someone that is going to give you a reference, and unfortunately, it has to be someone other than yourself.

Let's say that you choose not to use this approach when the question is asked, 'what are you doing now?' You will have to reply something like, "I haven't been doing any work for anyone else, I have been getting my CRC, my OSHA 10, my Certified Nursing Assistant (CNA Certificate)." There are some awesome things in that statement, but did they get past, "I haven't been doing any work for anyone else?" It's highly unlikely, huh?

Or maybe you haven't been working on the side for anyone. Then you might reply, "Well, I have 10 years' experience in Customer Service working at Sears and then Verizon, and I am finishing up my (Associate Degree, CRC, or professional certification). I am currently looking at several opportunities and trying to see who could use my help."

Now be honest, doesn't that sound so much better? The key is that you want to show a potential employer the value you have, what you bring to the table, and that you are constantly getting better. Does this make sense?

Criminal Record: You know the movie (all of them) where the boy meets a girl, and they fall in love... but he has a secret? He isn't exactly who she thinks that he is. He wants to tell her, but the timing is never right, then it all falls apart. Of course, you have; and in the movies, it always works out, but this isn't the movies, and when it comes to criminal records, the only 'right' time is at the beginning.

When filling out an application, if you have ever had a felony or misdemeanor, you **have** to give full disclosure. It does not matter if it was a DUI in 1979, or a bounced check 5 years ago that you had to go to court for, if it is on your background check, you have to disclose it.

Since you are applying for the job, it is safe to say that you are eligible to be employed, and because of this, *most* employers will not care. However, if you deny having a criminal record and it comes out, then the employer will be wary that you lied. They are also going to wonder what else you are hiding. Previously, we saw where human nature was an obstacle in regard to the word 'unemployed,' but here, it may actually work in the positive. Most people are in favor of 'second' chances, and they will root for the underdog. They may even want to be a part of your comeback story if you give them a chance to give you that opportunity.

If you have something that has gone through the legal system, realize that **background checks can go back 20-30 years,** so Full Disclosure is your only real option. You'd be surprised at how often it is disarming and even attractive to an employer, so embrace it! I've seen it work personally, remember the student I told you about in the introduction? I understand that this may be daunting, but everyone has made mistakes, most of us just don't have to carry them around on a sheet of paper or tell employers about them. However, you are still worthy of a job, and someone will be thrilled to hire you!

Fired or Let Go: The application will probably ask if you have ever been fired, let go, or dismissed. The answer to this question is **NO**.

"But Holly, they did let me go."

Your position was eliminated!

"But Holly, my position wasn't eliminated."

Yes, **your** position was eliminated, that's why you aren't working there any longer. Unless you were written up and were investigated, then your company **cannot** say anything negative about you. Even if you were fired, let go, or dismissed, all your former company can disclose, by law, is what your position was and how long you worked for them.

I have worked with literally hundreds of people who were fired for 'unjust' reasons (it happens) or because new management just wanted their own people. Others were let go because companies wanted to save money, and the employee's salary was too high. I have also worked with people who were fired for legitimate reasons, such as excessive tardiness, moral lapses, and the list goes on, but what they all have in common is that the employer cannot speak negatively about a former employee. It's against the law. They can only state that yes, you worked there and for how long. They aren't even allowed to disclose your salary if it is not public knowledge.

Now since we are endeavoring to paint an honest picture of the job search experience, we have to deal with the fact that not all employers are going to adhere strictly to the law, while others, if so inclined, may try to hinder your search in various ways. For instance, a savvy HR person may ask your former employer if you are eligible for rehire. This is the opportunity for the employer to torpedo your application, and they say, "No."

This is not the end!

There are still positive ways to respond to negative reports if they come up in an interview. You may want to reply, "I worked there for over 20 years, and they were able to hire two new employees for my salary. For them, it just made financial sense to go in another direction at this time."

However, let me caution you here, though it may be tempting, refrain from EVER saying anything negative about your former company. There is nothing wrong with moving on, but the new employer doesn't want to hear about your 'nasty' divorce, and more importantly, they don't want potentially disgruntled employees in their organization. You wouldn't want your date dragging up what a waste of space their former partner was on your first date, would you? All kinds of Red Flags there!

Here is what I want you to say instead, grab a pencil and take this down:

"THIS ECONOMY HAS AFFECTED A LOT OF REALLY GOOD PEOPLE, AND UNFORTUNATELY, I WAS ONE OF THEM."

There is no reason to assign blame or to assume it yourself. The truth is that it was a business decision, and you are moving on with a positive attitude. After all is said and done, that is all your prospective employer needs to know.

If the termination was with legitimate cause, you might simply take a more tactful response, "I had the opportunity to work there for (x amount of time), and I can say that I learned quite a bit from the experience and am excited about new challenges." People do understand that the work environment can be difficult and is often made up of some challenging people. How you handle the questions will likely make a larger impact than the report they received from a stranger.

Being unemployed is often one of the most frightening times of anyone's life, and losing a job is painful. I understand. It can leave you hurt, angry, ashamed, or all of the above. Let me assure you, there are amazing people just like you in this same boat. Most of us have been there at some point in time, but remember, you've been hired before, and you will be 'hired' again. So when they ask you why you are no longer there, simply respond, "I'm currently (finishing up my degree, taking certification classes, working on professional development) and taking the opportunity to explore several opportunities to see who can use my help."

The **Paradigm Shift** is how you 'think' about something, and that comes out in how you speak! In other words, there are two ways to 'think' about being unemployed... half empty and half full, and it truly does matter. Let's look at an example of the power of 'how we speak.'

Chick-fil-A is number 1 in Customer Service. What makes them different from all the other fast-food chains? What makes them better? More importantly, what makes them more attractive to their desired audience?

They say things differently.

A typical cashier may respond with, "you're welcome" if they say anything at all. Customer service representatives at Chick-fil-A actually say, "It was my pleasure." This little difference has an impact on people, it makes them feel good!

The way we think affects what we say as well as how we say it, and this frames the perception that others have of us. I hope to give you some key phrases that will allow you to make a positive impression on those that you talk with and leave them with a positive impression of you because perception is important. It's a significant reason as to why Chick-fil-A is the leader in customer service and a successful business.

Remember: Key phrases will affect how you are perceived by others, but perhaps, just as importantly, they can change how you perceive yourself. So the next time someone says," Have you found a job yet?' your answer is, "I am currently looking at several opportunities."

I am sure you are picking up on the theme!

The next time someone asks, "how come you no longer work there?" you respond, "I'm currently (finishing up my degree, taking certification classes, working on professional development) and taking the opportunity to explore several opportunities to see who can use my help."

You say it, and you keep saying it until you believe it.

Chapter Five Key Points:

The Resume: 3 Reasons to have a good one

1. It will be a lifesaver when filling out those extensive job applications.
2. A good resume will paint a picture of who you are much more effectively than a completed application package.
3. Branding: A resume is the backbone of your 30-second commercial.

Overcoming Elephants… How to talk about:

1. Gaps in employment.
2. Age.
3. Criminal Record.
4. Fired or 'Let go.'

Chapter Six

Listing References

WHO DO YOU KNOW?

A personal reference is the closest thing an employer can get to a guarantee regarding a potential employee. This is why the people you choose to list as references should be carefully considered.

Sure, the application asks for your last supervisor as a 'work' reference, but if you and your boss never got along, then don't put them down. Instead, list your boss's supervisor or someone else **in authority** with which you had a good rapport. This way, your prospective employer gets an accurate and honest assessment of your work, which is what they are looking for in the first place. Remember, your reference must be someone with authority, a co-worker will not suffice.

Note: If you are really worried someone is going to say something negative about you, it may be worthwhile to have someone call that employer for a reference check. If you find that they are saying things about you that are not factual, then that may be a lawsuit for defamation of character.

If you have owned your own business, then your customers should serve as your references.

Since being a student is a full-time job, it is acceptable for students to list faculty members for their references, such as a professor or advisor.

Board Members for any leadership or civic organization, such as the Rotary, Kiwanis, or United Way, could also serve as references if you volunteered with them, and they can speak to your work ethic.

There are four (4) things you need to know about references.

1. You only need three references.
   No matter how many years you have worked, you still only need three, and they must be professional not personal. Your mother, sister, cousin, or preacher will not do unless you have actually worked for them for money.

2. Ask before you list them!
   Before listing your references, you first need to ASK the person if they would mind being a reference for you. It is common courtesy.

3. Put them in the loop.
   Building on point #2... it is important to tell the person who is serving as your reference what type of job you are applying for. This allows them to be prepared for the phone call. Also, send them a copy of your resume. It might have been a while since the person has seen you or worked with you, so update them on what it is that you've done and what you are good at, it will help them sing your praises.

4. Know their information.
   A reference without contact information is not really a reference, now is it? Once you have verified someone will be your reference, make sure you have their updated information including:
   a. After their name, use the title and name of the company they worked for when you worked for them.
   b. Get a current Phone number and Email
   c. City and State
      You don't need to include a street address unless you want to, but you might want to include the City and State that someone lives in. (I had a retired Marine in my class, and one of his references was living in Dubai, but since he had a valid email, the reference was more than accessible and thus a viable option for him.)

Here is an example of a solid attachment for your references:

JOHN ROGERS

123 Main Street
Shelby, NC 28150
(704) 555-5555
RogersJohn@yahoo.com

REFERENCES

Name
Title
Company
Address
City, ST Zip
Phone
E-mail

Joe Smith
Biology Professor
Gardner-Webb University
Campus Box 5678
Boiling Springs, NC 28017
704-406-5555
Joe.smith@gardner-webb.edu

Jane Jones
Public Relations Coordinator
ABC Company
123 Main Street
Atlanta, GA 30305
404-651-5555
Jane.Jones@abc.com

Chapter Six Key Points:

Four things you need to know about references:

1. You only need three.
2. Ask before you list someone.
3. Keep them in the loop... let them know what jobs you are applying for.
4. Know their contact information.

Chapter Seven

Polish and Proofread

ORGANIZATION NOT ORGANISM

Since you probably needed a job yesterday, I can imagine that you are eager to take everything that we've gone over so far and hit the bricks. That is totally understandable, but there are few odds and ends that we need to consider, clean up, and put right before you do.

Basic formatting rules: We've discussed the 'content' of your resume pretty extensively so far, but it also needs to be grammatically correct and aesthetically pleasing as well. So I am going to give you a couple of tips for putting the best look on your resume.

1. Your name needs to be BOLD and usually in 20pt. font.
2. Your contact information should be done in 12pt. font, certainly no less than 10pt. It does not, however, need to be bold or large. Save the bold for the important information regarding your experience.
3. Note, never go below 10pt font on your resume.
4. Stay clear of crazy fonts. Times New Roman or Calibri are good standard fonts.

Emails & Phone Messages: Everyone loves a sense of humor, but there is a time and a place, and sometimes, discretion is the way to go. If your email is www.studmuffin@hotmail.com or sweetcheeks@gmail.com, you might consider setting up and listing a different email for your job search.

Also, make sure your phone message is appropriate. "Yo, you know what to do," doesn't convey professional communication skills and may dissuade potential employers from actually leaving a message. Also, you may love Eminem or Maroon 5, but the employer probably doesn't want to wait for the music to stop to leave a message.

While you are looking for a job, I suggest something like 'Hi, you've reached Joe/Jane Applicant, please leave a message, and I will get back to you as soon as possible. Thank you." You can change it back to "Yo," after you land the job, but until then, remember you are **branding** yourself, and your phone message should demonstrate the same professionalism as your resume.

If you haven't taken the time to set up your voicemail, then you are at risk of losing the hard work you've put into trying to secure an interview. If it's not set up, stop reading and set it up right now because, obviously, you've procrastinated too long already. I'll wait.

Proofreading: Your first interaction with the potential employer could be your resume application. If it's the resume, then have someone proofread it! You aren't concerned with their evaluation of your content, what you need is someone who can spell. They should check for capitalization, indention, word choice, and other grammatical issues that you may have missed. Often, when we try to proofread our own documents, we read what we want to see, what we intended to say, and not what we actually put down on paper.

For instance, while I was the Director of Career Services at Gardner-Webb University, I proofread a resume by a brilliant Computer Science major. He was a literal genius in almost every way. Still, he listed his Objective as: to work for a challenging **organism**.

Sure, it is clear that he meant to say **organization,** but in the end, he didn't, and he would have ended up showing a lack of attention to detail if he'd sent it out that way.

Another resume by a wonderful gentleman stated that he had, "17 years' experience working in **Hostility.**" Which I suppose could have been why he was seeking other employment, but more than likely, he meant Hospitality.

The worse by far was one of my Nursing students who said, and I quote, "Works well with the **pubic**." Yikes, it's amazing how important one little letter can be, and how much difference taking the time to have someone read behind you will make in the long run. She meant "the public." You send a message when you are careless with your resume, the wrong message. So please take my advice and proofread, then have someone else proofread your document behind you.

Chapter Seven Key Points:

3 things to remember before you send your resume or any professional correspondence:

1. Polish.
2. Etiquette.
3. Proofread.

Chapter Eight

Putting it Together

IT'S NOT STEALING

In this book, there are several examples that you can use as you work on your cover letter, resume, and references. I also have several examples on my website www.hopemotivationsuccess.com/resources or www.hollyhits.com, that you are welcome to use. This is not stealing. That is what they are there for, as long as what is on them actually relates to you. Don't list yourself as a CNA if you are not qualified. That's lying and generally frowned upon, not to mention they will notice if you pass out at the sight of blood.

I want you to take a moment and look over the next resume. Notice that it is a bit heftier than the ones we have worked with so far. Although it is preferable to condense your information onto one page, for some, it is just not possible. If this is the case, remember that employers don't 'read,' so keep the same mindset as if you were working with a single page. I would suggest not to go beyond a two-page resume.

Joe Smith II
♦ ♦ ♦
123 Northside ♦ Shelby, N. C. 28152 ♦ Phone: 704-123-1000
smithj@hotmail.com

As a seasoned and results-driven professional, I have a broad-based background as a technical manager, packaging production manager, maintenance supervisor and training coordinator. I have strong leadership and motivational skills; proven ability to quickly build rapport, establish trust, and train and motivate people of all levels. Recognized for professionalism, positive mental attitude, commitment to excellence and demonstrated ability to communicate and interact effectively with senior management, associates and customers. Big picture focus on company goals has produced increased efficiencies in production.

CORE COMPETENCIES:

- Team Building & Leadership
- Multi-Task Management
- Time and Resource Optimization
- Customer Needs Assessment
- Process Improvement
- ISO 9000 and 14000

- 19 Yrs. High-Speed Automation Experience
- Workflow Planning and Prioritization
- Quality Control Standards
- Creative Problem Solving
- Interviewing, Hiring, and Retention
- Team Member Training and Mentoring

COMPUTER AND TECHNICAL SKILLS:

- J. D. Edwards
- High Volume
- Word
- Ceridian

- High-Speed Automation
- PowerPoint
- Visio
- Kronos

- Word Perfect
- Excel
- MES

TRAINING/SEMINARS/WORKSHOPS

- 5S Workplace Organization
- Six Sigma (Green Belt)
- Internal Quality Auditing
- National Safety Council Training
- Building a Lean Culture
- Human Relations Skills Training
- Classroom Training Techniques
- Continuous Improvement

- Managing Multiple Projects, Objectives & Deadlines
- School of Fluid Powers
- Sexual Harassment Training
- Front Line Leadership – Zenger
- Miller
- Basic Supervision
- Basic Electricity
- Avoiding Litigation Land Minds

EDUCATION

Cleveland Community College, 1991-1993
Propulsion Engineering, 1985-1989
Boiler Water Testing
Fuel Oil Testing

College Transfer Program (Pre-Business)
Boiler Technician Class A School
Feed Water Testing
Gage Calibration

VOLUNTEER WORK

Ascension Lutheran Church, Chair of Finance, 2005

United Way Campaign Chairman, 2003

United Way

Day of Caring Property Co-Chair, 2002

PROFESSIONAL EXPERIENCE

ENTERTAINMENT DISTRIBUTION COMPANY   1989 to Present
Grover, North Carolina
Manager of Packaging (2005-present)
- Accountable for area safety, quality, and production of 850k compact disc/DVDs per day.
- Effectively manage/supervise 160-250+ production employees, including 5 production supervisors, 20 maintenance technicians, contact company personnel and one area engineer.
- Interpretation and administration of plant policy.
- Hiring of staff (operational, maintenance, and supervisory personnel).
- Responsible for area budgeting of $53 million.
- Adjust staffing requirements on a daily basis for employees based on production requirements.
- Management of Six Sigma projects.
- New customer integration.
- Developed significant improvements in layout and operational procedures to increase productivity.
- Spearheaded and lead strategies that improved processes resulting in cost savings of $125k quarterly.
- Initiated reduction of staffing, resulting in a cost savings of $132k annually.
- Implementation of Visual Workplace within the packaging department.
- Project $250k savings annually with process improvement.
- Cut 2% to 4% Scrap Cost Savings within one year.
- ISO auditors.

Assistant Manager of Packaging   *(2000 to 2005)*
- Responsible for area safety performance.
- Ensured overall area maintenance and equipment reliability.

UNIVERSAL MANUFACTURING
Grover, North Carolina

Area Support Engineer   (1999-2000)
Supervisor – Packaging   *(1993-1999)*
Maintenance Technician / Training Coordinator   *(1989 to 1994)*

MILITARY EXPERIENCE

United States Navy E4 – BT3 1985 USS Santa Barbara AE-28
- Boiler Technician
- Performed maintenance and overhaul of boilers, fuel oil service pumps and fire pumps and feed pumps (rotary screw, centrifugal and reciprocating)
- Fire Room Supervisor (Boiler Technician of the Watch)
  - Supervised watch personnel
  - Responsible for all operating equipment
- Calibration Supervisor
  - Supervised calibration personnel
  - Calibrated all shipboard pressure, vacuum, temperature gages and switches

Free, take one: As you glance over this resume, what stands out? Did you read the paragraph? It really is a good paragraph, but you're still not looking at it.

No, what your eyes go to are the headers; Highlights of Qualifications, Computer Skills, Education, etc. it's just natural. We gravitate toward the bold print and the bullets, and this is where we put the important stuff!

Now, I want you to start looking at resumes (visit www.hopemotivationsuccess.com and look under resources, you will find examples of all kinds of resumes), try to find ones that apply to your specific field. If you are in Customer Service, then pull that up, Nursing, Machinist, Teacher, whatever field you are qualified and start studying the bullet points they've used. Take note of which ones catch your eye. Notice how they articulated their experience or expertise, traits you may share, and incorporate them into your materials.

Note: please do not keep ANY information on a resume that is not applicable to you!

***These examples may also jog your memory of what you have done.

These are examples that I hope you will take advantage of; you don't have to reinvent the wheel.

Also, I want you to start looking up job responsibilities on www.indeed.com. (This information will be discussed in more details in Chapter 9.) If you want to see what employers want, then read what employers post under "job responsibilities," not qualifications. This method will help you describe what you have done with clear, concise bullets. When developing your resume, I would suggest you not look at the jobs that are posted locally but instead pull jobs from different cities. The point is for you to see how to describe what you have done under "job duties." When looking at www.indeed.com, you don't need to limit your search only by a job title. For example, in the "What" field of Indeed's search, if you are looking for a Customer Service Job, then just put the word "Customer" and see what jobs come up. If you are interested in "Social Work," just put the word "Social" or "Human" for Human Services in that "blank." You get the idea, explore Nursing, Machinist, Teacher, whatever field you are qualified for and start studying the bullet points they've used under job responsibilities. Take note of which ones catch your eye. Notice how they articulated their experience or expertise and incorporate them into your materials.

Education: Not all 'learning' leads to a cap and gown. You may have noticed that Robert's resume lists some college education but not a degree. Most of his learning was gathered through practical experience and on the job training. Employers want experience, and many of you have it even if you don't have an Associates or Bachelors.

If you have a certification, taken classes, or completed relevant courses, don't hesitate to list them on your resume! Examples include:

- Forklift Operator Certificate
- ISO 9000
- ISo 14000
- Six Sigma
- Yellow belt
- OSHA 10
- HIPPA COMPLIANCE
- CPR
- QUICKBOOKS
- HVAC

There are other items that are important in your particular field and should go on your resume. Things like the ACT National Career Readiness Certificate (CRC) if you have it.

(Unfamiliar with the CRC? For information about the CRC go to the official website: https://www.act.org/certificate/)

I am a firm believer in the CRC and always talk about it with the people I am working with, so let me give you my quick spiel. High school students can take a wide range of tests, including the SAT, GRE, LSAT, and MCAT. These test a student's aptitude and provide a good indicator of whether they will be successful in college, grad school, law school, or medical school. They are 'indicators.' Well, Business and Industry wanted a test to see how someone would do in the workplace. Please note, business and industry does not just mean manufacturing, this includes, healthcare, government, education, and various other industries.

So ACT created a test that is recognized nationwide called the CRC. This nationally recognized Certification process measures an applicant's aptitude in three specific areas.

1. <u>Locating Information:</u> This tests one's ability to extrapolate information from various sources, such as bar graphs and pie charts. Example: One graph might show Team 1 sold $3,200 worth of product, and team 2 sold

$3,400 worth of product. Based on the graphs you are looking at, who sold more products?

2. <u>Applied Math:</u> Now before you freak out, let me explain. It is important in any business that we have an applicable understanding of basic math. A question might be: If you have 10 trucks and they are driving 100 miles a day and gas is $4.50 a gallon, what would it cost to run these 10 trucks in a week? This is a practical application of math, not advance trigonometry or calculus.

3. <u>Reading for information</u>. This portion tests one's ability to read and comprehend basic instructions.

The Career Readiness Certification just shows the employer that you are job-ready regarding basic skills, and therefore, is a great thing to have listed on your resume. Also, some companies are beginning to use the CRC to evaluate employees for promotion.

How do you get a CRC? Community Colleges are usually the ones that have testing centers for the Career Readiness Certificate. They even offer a pre-test, no one see's your results but you, and then you can see where you need to skill up. At most locations, the Pre-Assessment and skilling up are FREE, so consider taking advantage of this awesome tool.

This is also a viable tool for Economic Development and Planning in the area. When employers are looking to relocate to a community or a local business or industry is looking to expand, they need to know if there is a viable workforce in the area that can do the work. The CRC is an incredible objective assessment that allows employers to understand the level of skills of that potential workforce.

Eureka: It is usually at this point in the class that my students have that 'Aha' moment where they begin to get it. They begin to recognize that they, in fact, do have skills and abilities that someone needs. They start to believe that a Paradigm Shift can indeed take place and that they should change the way they think and speak about themselves, their abilities, and their situation.

Why? Not because anything has changed but because we've pulled back the curtain and exposed what was always there. They **are** valuable because they **do** have skills, abilities, and experience that employers **want** and **need.**

"Yes," you say, "but I'm not comfortable going around just talking about how good I am."

Truthfully, most people aren't, but if you don't, who will? More importantly, if you don't tell them, how will they know you can fix their problem or meet their need? Let me tell you that they are more interested in filling their need than whether you are 'full of yourself.' It's not bragging if it's true, and if you can manage their human resource office, drive their school bus, mop their floor, or run their emergency room, then they will sing your praises as well.

Remember: Who needs what you do?

Someone does, I guarantee it. You are the **solution,** and that makes you **valuable**... to the person that has the **problem.** What's your real job in the job search? That's right, finding the person with the problem that you can fix.

Look at it like this, in America, water is abundant, and therefore, extremely affordable. We literally take it for granted. Imagine though that you lived in the desert, but on your property, there was a natural spring, an oasis if you will. You have plenty of water but no money. Then, along comes a man with a group of camels and horses who are hot, tired, and thirsty. He has a problem. He has no water, but what he does have is money. You, on the other hand, have no money but you've got all the water you need and then some.

Now, if the traveler recognizes that you have an abundance of water, **both** of your problems may be fixed! You will provide him with the answer to his problem in the form of the water **in exchange** for the answer to your problem in the form of the money that he will give you for your water.

Two important things for you to take hold of here. First, he must know what you have to recognize that you can fix his problem or meet his need. What he doesn't know can hurt you! Second, this is not charity. He is not doing you a favor. He is offering you a contract because he recognizes the value that you bring to the table. You are important!

This is a journey of opportunity, not a desperate search for help... because YOU are the HELPER. The employer needs you just as much as you need them.

So let's do a quick recap before we move onto the dreaded job application. It is a cold hard truth that 80% of jobs are obtained through some other process than answering a job posting. That is why it is important to get in front of the *right* people. You want to end up talking to the person who is authorized to hire you. Sure, you may need to talk to your friend Bob who works there to get the name of Nancy, who is the foreman's secretary, so that you can track down Joe the foreman. Trust me though, if Joe is in need of a heavy equipment operator, and you can shave the hair off a frog with a bulldozer, then he'll be glad that you did. Let the *right* people know what it is that you can do.

That is why working on your resume is so important. This is where you really think about who you are and what you've done up until this point. There are so many 'skills' that we perform every day that we just take for granted. Really consider all of the daily 'routine' things that you do, like the logs that you track your gas and mileage, that's Excel, and it's of value to most employers.

To give you an example, I had one student that, when asked what he did for his company, his response was: "Basically, I paint." Which was most certainly a true statement, but it wasn't all that he did.

Fortunately, his former manager was also attending the class and piped in, "Holly, he's not just a painter. He did the finishing work for our engines." Wait, he did what? It turns out that they had worked for a government contractor specializing in aerospace and that this painter had a *top-secret clearance*. It was his job to perform the quality assurance checks and finishing work on the engines, which did include painting, before they were shipped out. Really people, we have to do better at evaluating ourselves!

I looked at this guy and said, "Don't you ever tell me you are just a painter!" Because here's the thing, when you overlook what you've done, you paint a picture in someone else's mind that you aren't that valuable. "All I did was..." I tell you what it was, it was important, or they wouldn't have paid you for it, that's for sure.

What did the company do? What did they make? What was your part in that production? Was it an international company? When we think about our own job, we just do our job. What you see as routine, unimportant, and mundane, may be a matter of perspective because you've been doing it so long. If we are going to get the best out of your resume, you are going to have to really consider what you've actually done!

This process will also help you develop your 30-second commercial. Taking the time to consider all that you do and put it into a resume will help you clearly articulate it to Bob, Nancy, and Joe.

"Yes, but won't it sound rehearsed? Like I am trying too hard?"

This is important, so you should be trying hard, and I promise you that rehearsed and confident is so much more convincing than 'by the seat of your pants.'

Again, the best predictor of the future is past performance. That is why it is important that your resume is reflective of what you have done. When you have a well-developed resume, you will be able to fill out an application better, since it provides you with a one-sheet document with practically all of the information required to fill it out.

The Application: Even if you have a cover letter, resume, and a reference page, almost every company will want you to fill out their application for employment. It is a necessary evil, but congratulations, you do have a resume. Think of it as a cheat sheet for your application and use it.

I don't think we need to discuss how to answer most of the questions on the application. Your name, birthdate, social security numbers are all pretty self-explanatory. However, remember the tricky ones, such as 'have you ever been fired, let go, or dismissed?" The answer is emphatically, No. Unless you were fired for criminal or legal reasons (embezzlement, drug use, sexual assault, something that was written up and investigated), then you will have to say, "Yes." But that is a rare occasion. So please, most of you can just answer "No." Most applications have a section where they will ask why you left the previous job, and if it does, then the answer is that your position was 'eliminated.' You don't have to give a reason as to why it was eliminated, and you don't have to volunteer that someone else is now doing it.

As we stated before, a former employer can ONLY say what your position was and how long you worked there. They cannot say that you were fired. They can't even discuss your salary unless you give them permission or if it is a matter of state record. Technically, they can't even discuss whether you were a good or bad employee; they can only state your position and the duration of your employment.

I have consulted with a lot of professionals in Human Resources, and their advice to me is to tell my clients to say "NO" on an application when asked about being fired, dismissed, or let go. You can be dismissed for any reason or for no reason at all in many states, which is why this is such a subjective and unfair question.

This is what I want you to think about; are you a good employee, will you work hard; do you have a good work history? If so, then move forward. If a company or organization got rid of you, then you didn't need to work there.

If, on the other hand, the application asks if you've ever been convicted of a crime other than a traffic violation, and it usually does, then the answer is always 'Yes.' Honesty upfront is the only acceptable policy here. Even if the misdemeanor you have on your record took place 30 years ago, put it on the application. It is better to get the job with these cards clearly on the table than for them to come out during the interview process or later. Most employers value honesty and are willing to give you an opportunity if you give them a chance.

If your boss or direct supervisor was 'that guy' or 'woman,' then when the application asks for their name and number, you might consider other options. At first glance, this might seem wrong or even dishonest, but it's not. What the potential employer desires is to talk to someone in 'authority' who will give them untainted information. Your former supervisor, 'Biff,' isn't that person, so give them the name of his boss or maybe your executive director. The company will get the information they want, and you don't have to worry about someone being petty toward you.

What if the company no longer exists? Businesses go under all the time. There are major store closings, such as Kmart, Sears, or Goody's, where the entire staff, including managers, are let go. What do you do in an instance like this? Did the person you want to use as a reference die, or were they just let go? If they were just let go, then they are still a viable reference if you can find them. I suggest that you try locating them on LinkedIn, Facebook, or some other social networking platform. They are probably out there and would most likely be thrilled to give you a reference.

Just keep in mind that the name you give must be someone in authority that has knowledge of you as an employee. If you list your mom, well, that is not credible.

Last but not least, the application will ask for references. Remember that to be effective, they should be someone other than a relative, unless you have worked for a relative. Former supervisors, community leaders, and instructors are all potentially good references to use on an application.

Chapter Eight Key Points:

1. Don't reinvent the wheel... using a template is not stealing!
2. Utilize good verbiage; this will help you articulate what you have done.
3. A strong resume can help you fill out an effective application, make a great impression, and be a blueprint for your 30-second commercial.

Chapter Nine

Examining Different Types of Resumes

CHOOSE YOUR WEAPON

Job Search 102:

I was working with a woman who has worked extensively for NASA. I'll never forget waiting to meet Jo. She had degrees in Chemical, Industrial, and Mechanical Engineering, plus she had worked on the Space Shuttle! How cool is that?

In my mind, I had painted a picture of what this highly educated and accomplished woman must look like. She was, after all, a 'rocket scientist,' and therefore, must be bookish. I saw her in a plain blouse and pants, disheveled hair held up by a bright yellow #2 pencil, brown patent leather shoes, and glasses sitting cockeyed on the bridge of her nose. Oh, and the white lab coat that I assumed NASA issued to all of their employees as mandatory uniform apparel like hard hats on a construction site.

I was wrong.

Jo was not the 4'4" schoolmarm that I had naively imagined, but rather, a 5'6" athletic and extremely attractive woman with a lovely tan. Nor did she sport the trousers and lab coat of my imagination; instead, she wore a wide flowing skirt adorned with colorful flowers. She was the quintessential sun goddess, and I fear that my surprise showed on my face. I confessed somewhat guiltily as I shook her hand that she looked nothing like I had pictured her. She gently reminded me that NASA was not only in Florida but it was literally on the beach. Oh yeah, who knew?

What did not come as a surprise was the rich work history and experience that this accomplished woman brought with her. Her resume, all five pages of it, was written in detailed paragraph form. It was extensive and impressive. It was also much like *War and Peace*, worth the read but never checked out at the library. It also NEVER mentioned that she worked at NASA. Seriously? I'd have had that tattooed on my forehead if I had been her; you lead with that kind of information.

When I asked her why NASA wasn't in it, she explained, no one really works for NASA as it is mostly contract positions. "But did you help build the Space Shuttle," I asked?

"Yes," she replied, shrugging her shoulders a little.

"So NASA it is then," I said, "it's sexy, it sells, it's in."

"Do you have a security clearance?" was my next question.

Again, she answered, "Yes, of course."

"So that's sexy, it sells, it's in."

You do know what I mean by sexy, don't you? I mean it is information that draws your attention; it causes you to stop and take a second look. What information is going to draw an employer to your resume, so they know what you have done?

"Yes," you say, "but Holly, I never worked at NASA."

I hear you, I understand. However, not everyone is attracted by the same things. For instance, you may have graduated top of your class from John Hopkins Medical and are now the preeminent heart surgeon on the east coast, but no one is going to hire you to run heavy equipment. You just aren't sexy enough. Now Glen, whose skin is stretched like brown leather over his broad shoulders and who has been driving bulldozers and pans for the last 35 years, looks 'hot' on his resume! He's getting the job for sure. Why? Because he meets the needs of the company.

Let's take a look at Jo's resume.

Jo Rocket

1234 Lake Drive
Rockledge, FL 32955
jorocket@yahoo.com
(Secret Clearance – Inactive) CSTAR Eligible
(321) 123-1234

PROFILE

Motivated, high-energy, personable, business professional with a diverse background in the roles of logistics, project management, manufacturing and industrial engineer in **Aerospace, Defense and Commercial Industries**. Strong problem-solver who efficiently gathers and analyzes information by applying strong analytical skills and understanding of business processes, methodologies and the supply chain function. Consistently achieves business metrics of scheduling, cost, quality, and safety.

QUALIFICATIONS & ATTRIBUTES

Leadership Skills
- Resourceful self-starter, effective in researching and analyzing data.
- Program Development & implementation
- Motivating Leader and Trainer
- Flexible & versatile, maintains sense of humor under pressure

Logistics Engineer
- Logistics Planning & Supportability
- Liaison to NASA for United Space Alliance
- Troubleshooting/ Problem Solving
- Product/ Process Design
- Analytical and Highly Detail Oriented

Manufacturing/Industrial Engineer
- Project / Quality Management
- Process Optimizations utilizing LEAN concepts
- Engineering Design Calculations
- Training /Motivation/ Development
- Worked all aspects of manufacturing "from womb to tomb"

Organizational Skills
- Planning & Development
- Continuous Process Improvement
- Creative Problem Solver
- Championed innovative programs.

PROFESSIONAL HISTORY

Direct Labor

Logistics Engineer	*Space Shuttle Program*	United Space Alliance
Sr. Engineering Specialist	*Tomahawk & Advance Cruise Missile*	McDonnell Douglas,
Industrial Engineer/Production Planner	*Sonarbuoys*	Sparton Electronics Corp
Industrial Eng/Manufacturing Eng	*Electronic Cable Assemblies*	Belden Corp.

Contract Engineer Assignments

Sr. Industrial Engineer	*G200 Corporate Jet Completion Center*	Gulfstream Aerospace
Metrics Analyst	*Simulation software*	Lockheed Martin
Manufacturing Engineer	*G4 & G5 Corporate Jet Manufacturing*	Gulfstream Aerospace
Manufacturing Engineer/Planner	*C17 Aircraft Retrofit Program*	McDonnell Douglas
Sr. Industrial Eng/Production Planner	*Rock Crushing Plants*	Cedarapids, Inc. (Raytheon)
Industrial Engineer/Scheduler	*Joint Star program*	Northrop Grumman Corp.
Sr. Industrial Engineer	*Backhoe Tractors*	J. I. Case, Inc.

SKILLS SUMMARY

Logistics Engineer
Logistics Planning & Supportability/Avionics, Communication, Tracking and Pyros
- *Identified and resolved problems within the company supply chain and logistics operations regarding orbiter flight hardware through daily operations by supporting Lean Six Sigma initiatives.*
  - Served as a liaison to National Aeronautics and Space Administration (NASA) customer representing United Space Alliance (USA).
  - Presented briefings to Boeing, NASA, and USA leadership on high visibility projects and incidents regarding flight hardware to give status on part availability and mission-specific project status.

Jo Rocket

SKILLS SUMMARY (Continued)

- Coordinated and tracked flight material transfers between Kennedy Space Center (KSC) and certified repair facilities, ensuring timely, error-free repair and refurbishment of flight hardware.
- Researched, analyzed, and recommended solutions for Logistics Support Requests, eliminating loss of parts and sustaining operations.
- Managed inventory, condition, and repair processes on hardware for shuttle vehicles to ensure their flight readiness.
- Created and facilitated risk assessments and risk mitigation processes for space shuttle/orbiter parts.
- Utilized Enterprise Resource Planning (ERP) Systems to manage hardware status.
- Prepared and reviewed detailed operating procedures for submittal for the Original Equipment Manufacturer/Special Test Equipment (OEM/STE) Engineering group to ensure compliance with established safety and quality standards.
- Charted, prioritized, and tracked equipment for Manufacturing, Overhaul & Repair, ensuring successful purchases, receipt and installation of plant equipment.

Manufacturing/Industrial Engineer
- Redesigned, optimized & Set up (4) aircraft hangars per Lean concepts to increase flow from 4 aircraft to 6.
- Transitioned G200 aircraft product line to another facility 60 miles away. Generated plant, facility, back shop, and station layouts.
- Produced product flow, fixture design, and cost justification. Taught and implemented 5 S Plan. Developed methods, standard practices, and created a database for standardized planning. Scheduled software development, analyzed metrics, tracked cost and schedule performance, while providing management visibility through reports generated concerning shop performance and estimates of completion for meeting contract specifications.
- Developed on-line planning for sheet metal details and machined components, including tooling orders, special materials purchases, and incorporated engineering changes.
- Coordinated with manufacturing production to resolve tooling problems and production difficulties. Generated interior trim, structural modifications, and avionics production planning

Industrial Engineer
- Worked all aspects of manufacturing "from womb to tomb." Developed detailed assembly instructions, visual aids, determined all parts, material, and tooling requirements for production.
- Developed manufacturing layouts (facility & station) and synchronized new design into production.
- MRP II start-up team, process mapping, tracked inventory problems, ordered special materials, and performed cost forecasting. Engineered tooling, jig, and fixtures to improve production, quality and reduce cycle time. Part of Integrated Product Team, developed the engineering, manufacturing and tooling basic release for assembly fabrication, installation and checkout.
- Worked pilot builds using videos and pilot build operators to generate methods, workflow instructions, tooling requirements, station layouts, product handling, and balanced product line flow while using Computerized M.O.S.T. (Maynard Operational Sequenced Technique – a predetermined motion system) to generate incentive production standards.
- Established and maintained Industrial Engineering Department at Belden's Gastonia, NC plant. Wrote procedures, performed audits, established and maintained incentive production standards.
- Developed production methods, ergonomics studies, and OSHA requirements. Generated shop practices, product flow, job design, and facility optimization.
- Implemented Safety program and training; **Won NC State Industry Safety Award.**

EDUCATION & SPECIALIZED TRAINING

Bachelor of Science, Liberal Arts University of New York
Associate Degree, Industrial Engineering Technology, Gaston College
Associate Degree, Mechanical and Production Engineering Technology, Gaston College

United Space Alliance Leadership Development Institute Series
Certificate APICS Supply Chain Management
Blue Card Certified in M.O.S.T. and Maxi M.O.S.T. (predetermined motion system)
Certified MOST Instructor (Maynard Operational Sequenced Technique)

*Take a look at her first paragraph. Notice what we did to make certain your eyes were going to go to the ***right*** words. We italicized and put Aerospace, Defense, and Commercial Industries into bold font.

PROFILE

Motivated, high-energy, personable, business professional with a diverse background in the roles of logistics, project management, manufacturing and industrial engineer in ***Aerospace, Defense, and Commercial Industries***. Strong problem-solver who efficiently gathers and analyzes information by applying strong analytical skills and understanding of business processes, methodologies and the supply chain function. Consistently achieves business metrics of scheduling, cost, quality, and safety.

QUALIFICATIONS & ATTRIBUTES

---

*Then we added the quadrants: Leadership, Logistics Engineer, Manufacturing Engineer, and Organizational Skills.

QUALIFICATIONS & ATTRIBUTES

Leadership Skills
- Resourceful self-starter, effective in researching and analyzing data.
- Program Development & implementation
- Motivating Leader and Trainer
- Flexible & versatile, maintains sense of humor under pressure

Manufacturing/Industrial Engineer
- Project / Quality Management
- Process Optimizations utilizing LEAN concepts
- Engineering Design Calculations
- Training /Motivation/ Development
- Worked all aspects of manufacturing "from womb to tomb"

Logistics Engineer
- Logistics Planning & Supportability
- Liaison to NASA for United Space Alliance
- Troubleshooting/ Problem Solving
- Product/ Process Design
- Analytical and Highly Detail Oriented

Organizational Skills
- Planning & Development
- Continuous Process Improvement
- Creative Problem Solver
- Championed innovative programs

Take a look at some of the bullets in these quadrants:

- Troubleshooting/ Problem Solving
- Continuous Process Improvement
- Project Management
- Quality Management

Folks, remember that you have access to these resumes, and you can use some of these bullets as well as the phrasing in these resumes, just pick the information that is relevant to you and what you have done. The point is that you can get inspiration from examining different types of resumes to determine what suits you best.

Now Jo's resume is a little different under Professional History because she had a lot of contracts. Still, we allotted enough space in this area for her to detail where she worked and what she did.

PROFESSIONAL HISTORY

Direct Labor

Logistics Engineer	*Space Shuttle Program*	United Space Alliance
Sr. Engineering Specialist	*Tomahawk & Advance Cruise Missile*	McDonnell Douglas,
Industrial Engineer/Production Planner	*Sonarbuoys*	Sparton Electronics Corp
Industrial Eng/Manufacturing Eng	*Electronic Cable Assemblies*	Belden Corp.

Contract Engineer Assignments

Sr. Industrial Engineer	*G200 Corporate Jet Completion Center*	Gulfstream Aerospace
Metrics Analyst	*Simulation software*	Lockheed Martin
Manufacturing Engineer	*G4 & G5 Corporate Jet Manufacturing*	Gulfstream Aerospace
Manufacturing Engineer/Planner	*C17 Aircraft Retrofit Program*	McDonnell Douglas
Sr. Industrial Eng/Production Planner	*Rock Crushing Plants*	Cedarapids, Inc. (Raytheon)
Industrial Engineer/Scheduler	*Joint Star program*	Northrop Grumman Corp.
Sr. Industrial Engineer	*Backhoe Tractors*	J. I. Case, Inc.

SKILLS SUMMARY

Your eyes can easily take in: Logistic Engineer, Space Shuttle Program, Gulfstream Aerospace, Metrics Analyst, and Sr. Industrial Engineer.

Is it everything that this amazing woman had ever done? Of course not, but keep in mind that resumes DO NOT get you the job, they only get you the interview. Therefore, we don't have to pack everything in, just the information that makes you interesting enough to the potential employer.

Let me point out something else, numbers and acronyms draw attention. An employer may not read the words National Aeronautics and Space Administration, but NASA sure stands out. For instance, if I said that I worked for the National Security Agency, most people wouldn't be impressed, but if I said I worked for the NSA, most people would take notice. It's the same place, but how we say it, or in this case write it down, makes a difference.

Manufacturing Engineer	*G4 & G5 Corporate Jet Manufacturing*	Gulfstream Aerospace
Manufacturing Engineer/Planner	*C17 Aircraft Retrofit Program*	McDonnell Douglas
Sr. Industrial Eng/Production Planner	*Rock Crushing Plants*	Cedarapids, Inc. (Raytheon)
Industrial Engineer/Scheduler	*Joint Star program*	Northrop Grumman Corp.
Sr. Industrial Engineer	*Backhoe Tractors*	J. I. Case, Inc.

SKILLS SUMMARY

Logistics Engineer
Logistics Planning & Supportability/Avionics, Communication, Tracking and Pyros
- *Identified and resolved problems within the company supply chain and logistics operations regarding orbiter flight hardware through daily operations by supporting Lean Six Sigma initiatives.*
  - Served as a liaison to National Aeronautics and Space Administration (NASA) customer representing United Space Alliance (USA).
  - Presented briefings to Boeing, NASA, and USA leadership on high visibility projects and incidents regarding flight hardware to give status on part availability and mission-specific project status.

If you have worked for over 20 years, refrain from putting down the actual number. Example: If you've worked in the field for 32 years, simply put 20+ years. It's impressive, and sometimes less is more.

When writing the number of years, always use the actual number versus spelling the number out. Numbers are easier to read when skimming, plus they are sexier.

When writing your bullets, make sure you are quantifying the information.

Example:

- decreased wastes by 15%.
- generated 25% revenue.

Use actual numbers to draw attention to what it is you have done. If you have worked on a multi-million-dollar project, write it out 10 Million.

As you can see by looking at these resumes, you are not completely reading, you are looking at headers, numbers, what is bold or italicized. Most people skim, they don't read, and even in a bullet point, most people only read the first 3 words. That is why it is so important to use action verbs: See the list of action verbs listed on the next page.

ACTION VERBS:

Analysis
Abstracted
Analyzed
Appraised
Assessed
Briefed
Clarified
Classified
Compared
Computed
Correlated
Critiqued
Debated
Defined
Determined
Diagnosed
Discriminated
Dissected
Evaluated
Examined
Identified
Inspected
Integrated
Interpreted
Interviewed
Investigated
Judged
Maintained
Mapped
Monitored
Observed
Perceived
Ranked
Read
Reasoned
Related
Researched
Reviewed
Screened
Scanned
Solved
Studied
Summarized
Surveyed
Symbolized
Verified
Visualized

Assistance
Advised
Assisted
Bolstered
Collaborated
Contributed
Consulted
Cooperated
Enlisted
Facilitated
Fostered
Helped
Participated
Referred
Served
Strengthened
Supported
Sustained

Communication
Addressed
Advertised
Answered
Briefed
Communicated
Corresponded
Debated
Explained
Expressed
Facilitated
Interpreted
Interviewed
Lectured
Listened
Narrated
Prepared
Presented
Publicized
Recorded
Responded
Spoke
Talked
Wrote

Creation and Development
Acted
Adapted
Authored
Bolstered
Built
Charged
Clarified
Composed
Conceived
Corrected
Created
Designed
Developed
Devised
Discovered
Drafted
Eliminated
Established
Expanded
Expedited
Experimented
Facilitated
Fashioned
Fixed
Formulated
Generated
Improved
Increased
Influenced
Initiated
Innovated
Instituted
Integrated
Introduced
Invented
Launched
Modified
Originated
Perceived
Performed
Planned
Prioritized
Produced
Promoted
Recommended
Reduced
Restored
Refined
Revamped
Set
Shaped
Simplified
Solved
Styled
Streamlined
Substituted
Visualized

Achievement
Advanced
Allowed
Assured
Bolstered
Eliminated
Encouraged
Expanded
Facilitated
Fostered
Guaranteed
Improved
Increased
Inspired
Mastered
Maximized
Minimized
Motivated
Obtained
Overcame
Promoted
Provided
Reduced
Restored
Stimulated
Strengthened
Upgraded

Teaching and Counseling
Adapted
Advised
Advocated
Aided
Applied
Assessed
Assisted
Bolstered
Briefed
Cared
Charged
Clarified
Coached
Comforted
Communicated
Conducted
Consulted
Coordinated
Demonstrated
Educated
Emphasized
Enabled
Encouraged
Enlightened
Established
Exercised
Explained

Facilitated	Implemented	Correlated	Purchased
Fostered	Installed	Detailed	Raised
Guided	Modified	Developed	Recommended
Helped	Ordered	Facilitated	Recruited
Implemented	Prepared	Filed	Stimulated
Improved	Prioritized	Gathered	
Influenced	Produced	Graphed	**Supervision and**
Informed	Programmed	Identified	**Management**
Inspired	Promoted	Inspected	Administered
Interpreted	Ran	Located	Allocated
Investigated	Reduced	Maintained	Approved
Lectured	Repaired	(Records)	Arranged
Led	Serviced	Mapped	Assigned
Listened	Set	Met (Deadlines)	Authored
Maintained	Sustained	Stimulated	Bolstered
Manipulated	Transported		Coached
Modified	Upheld		Conducted
Motivated	Used	**Service**	Contracted
Observed	Utilized	Assisted	Controlled
Perceived	Negotiation	Attended	Decided
Persuaded	Advised	Cared	Delegated
Promoted	Advocated	Catered	Directed
Read	Arbitrated	Delivered	Dispatched
Reduced	Bargained	Entertained	Distributed
Reflected	Expedited	Facilitated	Educated
Reinforced	Facilitated	Furnished	Encouraged
Related	Lobbied	Listened	Enforced
Restored	Medicated	Maintained	Evaluated
Saved	Merged	Prepared	Executed
Shared	Motivated	Procured	Exercised
Solved	Negotiated	Provided	Expedited
Spoke	Persuaded	Satisfied	Facilitated
Stimulated	Promoted	Served	Fired
Strengthened	Reconciled	Supplied	Followed (Through)
Substituted	Soled		Fostered
Supported		**Persuasion**	Hired
Sustained	**Organization**	Aide	Implemented
Taught	Accumulated	Advertised	Instructed
Trained	Arranged	Auctioned	Led
Validated	Assembled	Bartered	Maintained
	Balanced	Bolstered	Managed
Operations and	Budgeted	Enlisted	Met (Deadlines)
Repairs	Built	Facilitated	Monitored
Adjusted	Cataloged	Generated	Motivated
Adapted	Clarified	Helped	Organized
Bolstered	Classified	Improved	Oversaw
Clarified	Collated	Led	Planned
Corrected	Collected	Maintained	Prepared
Eliminated	Compiled	Motivated	Prioritized
Expedited	Composed	Negotiated	Promoted
Facilitated	Coordinated	Persuaded	Purchased
Fixed	Copied	Promoted	

Don't forget that these resumes are available to you at the website: www.hopemotivationsuccess.com/resources

Feel free to download and use these materials. These are Word documents, so you save them to your desktop or flash drive and then pick which format you like, rename it, and then modify it with YOUR information. Simple.

Please make sure you put your information, do not say that you can do something that you can't do. Everything on your resume needs to be true, and you need to be able to talk about it.

Note: The average employer looks at a resume for 15-30 seconds. So the question you need to ask yourself is what information can the employer 'see' on your resume that will let them know what you have done, what you are capable of doing, and how you can help them. When you glance over your resume, do you come away with the right impression? If not, keep working at it until you do.

Not yet a Rocket Scientist? For those of you who don't have a lot of experience, let me show you my daughter's resume. This is one that we put together while she was still in high school. I know what you're thinking; I don't look old enough to have adult children. True, but I actually have two; a boy and a girl, and they are twins! Let me just say, I am incredibly proud of my son and daughter!

Okay, back to the resume stuff. When my daughter was applying for college, she was interested in schools that had a nursing program, even as a 17-year-old, you can get an idea of her passions.

Taylor G. Sweat

111 Twin Lake Drive
Shelby, NC 28150

tay_g123@yahoo.com

Home: (704) 434-1234
Cell: (704) 444-1234

OBJECTIVE

Attend Baylor University for Nursing

QUALIFICATIONS & ATTRIBUTES

Leadership Skills

- Resourceful self- starter
- Motivate and Encourage others
- Disciplined & Strong work-ethic
- Takes initiative, strong problem-solver
- Won the "Celebrate Liberty Essay Contest" for North Carolinas State Lion's Club

Sports

- Cheerleader (8 Years)
  - Won Sportsmanship Award
  - Cheer Captain
- Track (3 years)
  - 800 meter
  - 4x800 meter relay

Clubs/ Organizations

- All-State Baptist Youth Choir
- National Honor Society
- Beta Club
- Future Business Leaders of America
  - Secretary (2 years)
- Fellowship of Christian Athletes
- Drama Club
- Year Book Club

Community Involvement

- Vacation Bible School
  - Assistant Teacher
  - Recreation Leader
- Mission Trips (Nashville, NY, Memphis, Philadelphia, Canada, Boston, and Charleston)

EDUCATION

THOMAS JEFFERSON CLASSICAL ACADEMY
Graduation May 2013
Honors Student
(Thomas Jefferson Classical Academy ranked top 1% in the Nation for Public Charter Schools)

WORK EXPERIENCE

2007- Present	*Babysitter*	**Certified Safe Sitter**, Cleveland Regional Medical Ctr. Shelby, NC
Summer 2012	*Packaging*	**Alive Apparel,** Print Company, Fallston, NC
Summer 2012	*Camp Counselor*	Camp Loy White, First Baptist Church, Shelby, NC
Summer 2011	*Healthcare Camp*	Code Teen, Cleveland Regional Medical Center, Shelby

HEALTHCARE EXPERIENCE

CODE TEEN CAREER CAMP   Summer 2012
Cleveland Regional Medical Center, Shelby NC

- Job Shadowing:
  - Emergency Department – Round with a registered nurse taking a room assignment in the Emergency Department.
  - Occupational Therapy – Help adult and pediatric patients adapt activities and use adaptive equipment.
- Learned about and visited the following areas of the Hospital:
  - Ob/Gyn Unit
  - Operating Room
  - Intensive Care
  - Physical Therapy
  - Occupational Therapy
  - Laboratory
  - Cardiopulmonary
  - Radiology
  - Respiratory Therapy

REFERENCES AVAILABLE

Do you get an idea of what this kid is like? Absolutely, you can, it's all listed on her resume: Leadership, sports, cheerleader, track, Future Business Leaders of America, Fellowship of Christian Athletes, Missions. Has she worked? Yes, even as a babysitter, she went to the local hospital and got a safe sitter certificate where she learned CPR and the Heimlich maneuver. She went above and beyond what was asked of her.

She also did an internship in a hospital, where she was able to experience surgery, radiology, as well as occupational therapy. So if she is applying to Nursing School, do you have an idea if she'll like it? Absolutely, she has already been exposed to it and still wants to do it.

She came home after her internship and said, "Mom, I even like the smell of the hospital." What? Thank goodness God creates people to like different things. Do you see how reading her resume gives you a picture of what someone might be like or capable of?

What does YOUR resume say about you?

Changing canoes in the middle of the stream? There are many who, for one reason or another, decide they need a change. This can be terrifying, but it can also be the best decision a person can make in their lives. After all, your career is an extension of yourself, and thus, it is beneficial if you like what you do.

Since you are going to spend the lion's share of your life at work, it is important to be doing something you enjoy. So often, I work with people who are looking for work but would rather take a nail to the forehead than to go back into their previous line of employment. I get it!

So don't try to get a job in that area. If there is a job you don't like, you won't really be good at it, and if you are, you won't be happy with it, and if you aren't happy, you surely won't stay with it. Then you will be right back here trying to find another job.

I worked with a client who had 24 years' experience as a Product Manager in manufacturing. He was extremely hirable in his field, but what he wanted to do was teach.

"Are you sure, you know that would be working with kids, are you sure you would like that?" I asked. Let's face it, not everyone is a kid type of person. It takes a special kind of grace to work in education.

"How do you know that it will fit you?"

He conveyed to me that he had been volunteered as a tutor and mentor for several years and loved it. However, there was nothing on his resume that indicated anything other than manufacturing. Friends, you can catch the right fish with the wrong bait.

Of course, he had no real Work Experience to support his desire for the new career, but he did have **Relevant Experience**, and we got busy listing it on his resume. We highlighted the fact that he had volunteered with a local non-profit to provide tutoring and mentorship as well as the ages of the students that he worked within this capacity. We stressed his proficiency in subjects, such as math and English, and even his experience developing student programs. We put his best foot forward in his job search.

BLET: I have found that there are a great number of people who decide to make a career change into law enforcement. It is not unusual for my Basic Law Enforcement Training students to have been welders, machinists, or even customer service personnel before enrolling. So why would they make good candidates for law enforcement? Let's take a look at how we can show transferrable skills on a resume:

Paul Police
❖ ❖ ❖
641 Prison Road ❖ Kings Mountain, N C 28086 ❖ Cell: 704-734-3333
Policeofficer@carolina.rr.com

POLICE OFFICER

COURSE STUDY:

- Crime Prevention Techniques
- Domestic Violence Response
- *Rapid Deployment*
- Controlled Substance
- Subject Control/ Arrest Techniques

- Search & Seizure, Technical Surveillance
- Narcotics, Domestic Violence, Felonies
- Leadership/ Teambuilding
- Workflow Planning and Prioritization
- Law Enforcement Driver Training

- Firearms
- Anti-Terrorism
- Patrol Techniques
- Arrest Techniques
- Crowd Management

CERTIFICATIONS:

- *OSHA Certification*
- Black Belt in Karate
- BLET Certification
- Counter-Terrorism (Tier 3)

- OC Spray Certified
- PPCT Certified
- CPR/ First Aide, First Responder
- *HAZMAT*

- Crime Prevention Certification
- Radar Certification
- MDT/DCI Certification
- *Interior Structural Firefighting*

HIGHLIGHTS OF QUALIFICATION

- Constantly monitored the quality of product during the production process
- Demonstrated problem-solving skills by helping minimize downtime
- Coordinate/perform designated materials management activities, including Inventory Control; placing orders with vendors; Receiving incoming orders; Stocking, rotating, and maintaining inventory.
- Process and maintain materials management records and files, including purchase orders, receivers, invoices, packing slips, open and close
- Pick supplies and equipment for orders as indicated on the shipping order.
- Assemble, package and coordinate deliveries for commercial carriers, such as Federal Express and United Parcel Service deliveries.
- Perform designated hazardous waste management and disposal activities and maintain records as required.
- Performed loading and unloading trucks.
- Transported shipment to particular areas by the forklift or other tools.
- Received, unpacked, and checked arriving shipments with demand Stock storage services.

PROFESSIONAL EXPERIENCE

2014-Present	**BLET STUDENT**	*Pitt Community College,* Greenville, NC
Apr 2007- 2014	**MACHINIST**	**Baldor/ ABB**, Kings Mountain, NC
Feb 2001 Apr. 2007	**FIRST CLASS WINDER**	*PPG Industries,* Shelby, NC

MILITARY

United States Marine Corp *Security Guard/Logistics Supply Clerk*   1981-1988

EDUCATION

Pitt Community College, Greenville, NC
Basic Law Enforcement Training, 2014

It is apparent, on their resume, that they have some of the important skills sets that are going to make them marketable as police officers such as:

- Constantly monitor the quality of products. (Vigilance is a vital trait for a police officer. They must be constantly aware of what is going on around them. So yes, this is a transferable skill.)
- Demonstrated problem-solving skills. (Another transferable skill.)
- Material management (Ability to ensure you have all the necessary materials to do your job.)

Do you see how you can write things as a "Transferable skill"? So now, let's take a look at how to write your transferable skills.

Populating your resume: How many of you are familiar with www.indeed.com? If you are not, you need to write this down. This is a job search engine that pulls from Career Builder, Monster, Hot Jobs, and various other internet job search sites.

It is also a FREE search engine.

> SPECIAL NOTE: There are enough great sites and resources out there that are FREE. You DO NOT need to pay for services to have an effective Job or Career Search.

Often though, people don't get the most out of using Indeed.com because they don't know how to navigate it properly. So let's do it together.

On the front page of the website (we will refer to it as the search engine from this point forward), it has a box titled "What."

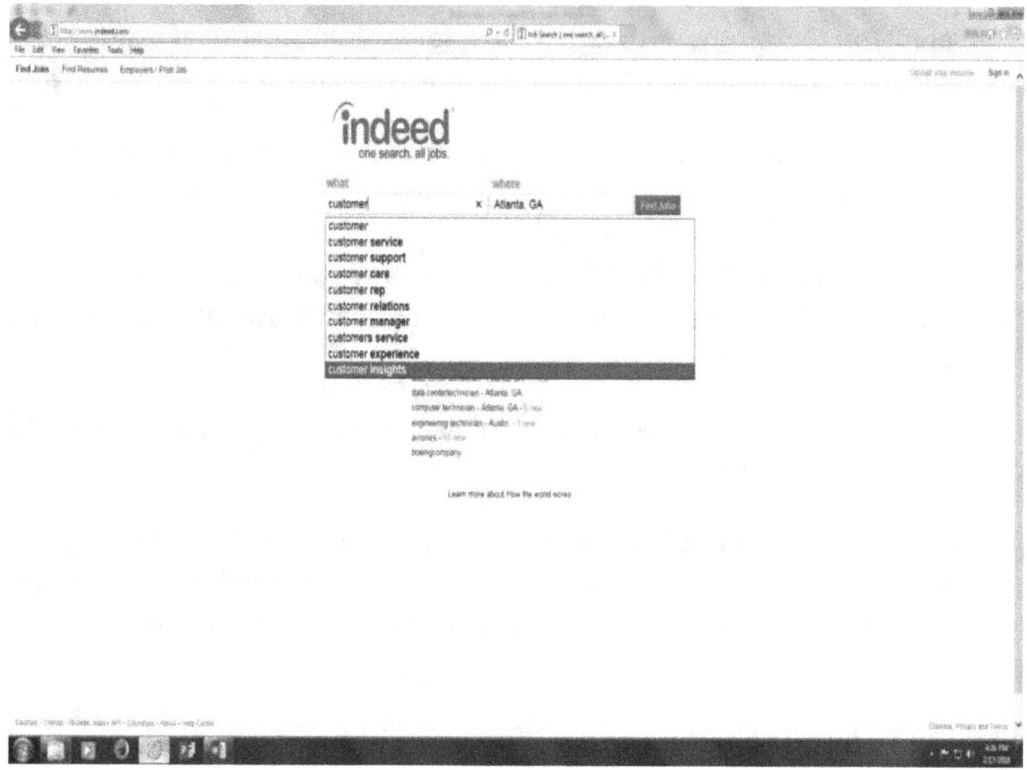

This is referring to 'what' type of job or job title you are interested in. So if you are interested in being a Customer Representative, this is where you would enter that in. However, let me suggest that we only use the first word of the job title. So in this instance, we would just type in 'Customer.' Doing it this way will give us all the positions listed that are associated with the term customer. Of course, you can narrow the results by adding 'representative' if you chose.

If you do "Office Administration," just put the word "Office" at first to get an idea of all the positions related to that field.

For those who have worked in a Warehouse, you might want to put just the word "Shipping" and see what comes up.

Here is an example of a search for the word 'office.' Notice the variety of postings. You can also see that they have entered in the geographical area that they desired to search. This search returned 72 new listings for the job applicant.

SECRETS OF LANDING THE JOB

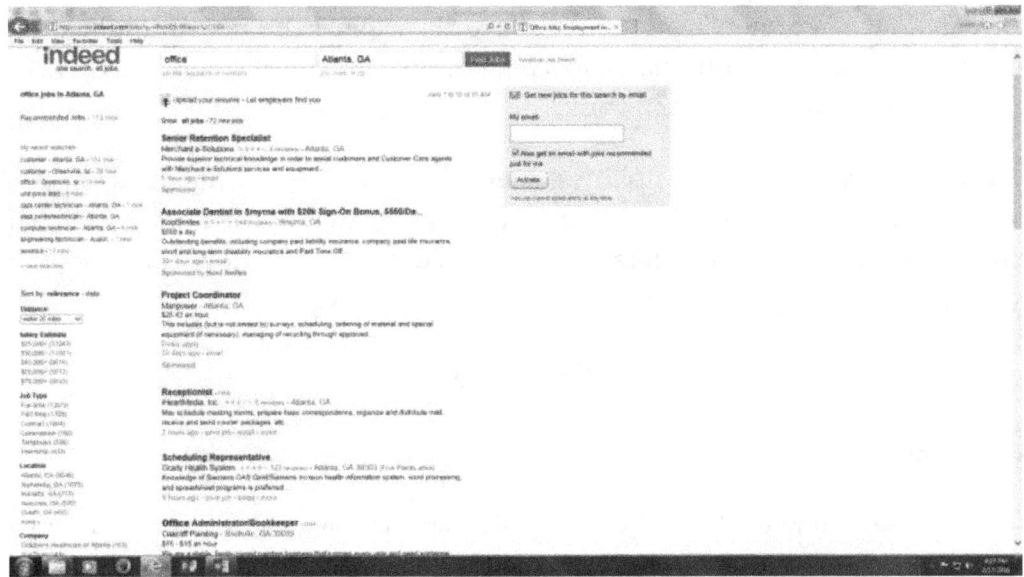

At this point, you might remember that I said 80% of the jobs that are hired are not gotten from job postings. Then why are we looking at the Internet? There are actually three good reasons:

1. This helps you see what companies are out there and what they are looking for.
2. It helps you identify titles of jobs that you may not have considered looking up that are similar to what you have done.
3. This is Key...You can see the knowledge, skills, and abilities that employers are looking for in these types of jobs.

Now, watch this, how do YOU populate your resume with exactly the right verbiage that describes the responsibilities for the jobs you held? How do you identify the skills you need to have for the job you want to have? I am about to show you how to design your resume with the very things that employers are looking for.

When you are on www.indeed.com, start your search in a different geographical location than the one that you desire a job in. If you live in Greenville, NC, put in Greenville, SC, then put in the one word that will describe what you are looking for or that you have done, such as 'Customer' for customer service.

Now I want you to click on some of those jobs and read the "responsibilities" instead of the qualifications. The qualifications are going to say that the candidate needs 5 years' experience, a BA in Basketweaving, or their own transportation. This absolutely isn't important because we aren't interested in any of that. What we are looking at is the employer's list of what is required for the position. This is valuable information. It's like knowing a woman's favorite cologne and restaurant before the first date. It's information that you can use to get noticed and make a good impression. It's doing your homework.

As you look over the responsibilities, you will inevitably recognize a lot of the things you have done. I want you to go ahead and highlight the information, copy it, then paste it to a word document. We will use it later. For now, take a look at a few examples.

Example:

Essential Functions

- Receives and responds to all customer inquiries and complaints that may pertain to all phases of operations, including membership, billing, orders, and changes to mailing lists.
- Records all customer contacts, including resolution or forwarding action taken to refer the question to the proper party.
- Whenever possible, resolves questions directly so that the customer receives prompt satisfaction (goal is to never transfer any customer more than once).
- Explains contract terms accurately in simple language so that the customer can understand the explanation and how it applies to the particular question.
- Responds promptly to all written inquiries or notifies the customer if there will be a delay in obtaining a final resolution to the problem.
- Takes note of recurring questions or problems that may be resolved or alleviated by changes in policy or procedures.
- Responsible for soliciting out of office information and updating calendar on p drive.
- Performs other related duties as required.
- Updates SMC³ Customer and prospect list.
- Maintain CRM Database.
- Handles ACD (automated call distribution system) calls routed to Customer Service.
- Responsible for coordinating/prioritizing tasks on a daily basis.
- Handles annual licensing renewal – tracking and maintenance.
- Maintains business relationships with small and medium-size accounts seeking guidance and direction from assigned supervisor and/or Sales.

These are the functions that were in a job description for a customer service position, now you can modify the bullets with your information.

Example:

- Received and responded to customer inquiries and complaints that pertained to all phases of operations, including membership, billing, orders, and changes to mailing lists.
- Recorded all customer contacts, including resolution or forwarding action taken.
- Resolved questions directly so that customers received prompt satisfaction.
- Explained contract terms accurately in a simple language so that customers could understand the explanation and how it applied to their particular question.
- Promptly responded to written inquiries.
- Responsible for soliciting out of office information and updating calendar.
- Updated SMC³ Customer and prospect list.
- Maintained CRM Database.
- Handled ACD (Automated Call Distribution system) calls routed to Customer Service.
- Responsible for coordinating/prioritizing tasks on a daily basis.
- Handled annual licensing renewal – tracking and maintenance.
- Maintained business relationships with small and medium-size accounts seeking guidance and direction from assigned supervisor and/or Sales.

Wow, isn't this exciting! For my clients who say, "I don't know how to describe what I did," this makes it simple and effective.

Look at other jobs; see exactly what employers want you to do, and if you have done what the job description is describing. If so, copy it then modify it using the proper tense (past tense, or present tense), quantify the information (Ex: saved the company 12% on waste material), and you will have a resume that describes exactly what the employer needs.

Using www.indeed.com, go and search terms like machinist, electrician, sales, manager, technician, social worker, principal, financial advisor, food services and get a feel for how to use this tool.

Chapter Nine Key Points:

Resume Tips

1. Identify the skills the employer values.
2. Remember, employers don't actually Read, they Skim (15-30 seconds maximum).
3. Bullet points are our friends.
4. Don't be afraid to get help... Indeed.com is excellent to help populate your resume.

Chapter Ten

Beyond the Resume

BODY OF EVIDENCE

Studies show that body language or non-verbal cues account for over 50% of our in-person communication. This is substantially more than words and tone of voice combined. In fact, just roll your eyes, and you'll send a silent but very clear message. Conscious or not, body language often reveals what we are thinking and feeling, and a good interviewer will notice. Your resume may be beyond reproach, but are you as impressive in person as you are in print?"

Dress for Success: Clothing is non-verbal communication. Clothes say a lot about you. They speak to your values, economic status, self-awareness, and more. So when interviewing, how you dress will make an impression on your potential employer, so keep it professional and appropriate.

Of course, not everyone will be interviewing for IBM or Apple, but it is important to make sure that you always present yourself in a clean fashion. It is best to avoid frayed, wrinkled, or soiled clothing for an interview regardless of the job you are applying for. It is also good to be cautious about clothes that are baggy, tight, too short, revealing, or trendy. Times are changing, but modesty is still a very valuable commodity in most of the business world.

If you are worried about expenses, let me set your mind at ease, you can put together good interview outfits without breaking the bank. Now money isn't as tight for me as it once was, but I am still not afraid to shop at Goodwill. I am an avid 'treasure' shopper, have been for years, and people have always complimented me on my style. If they only knew that I picked up my *Jones of New York* for $7.00 at the thrift store. Don't overlook Goodwill, the Salvation Army, Ross, or Marshalls because they are discount stores. There is no reason to spend more money on what you like than you have to. It's just good sense.

Dressing appropriately not only gives you credibility, it surrounds you with a sense of belonging that can help deflect the minor slips or stumbles that we all make during that critical interview, or once hired, in daily routines.

One of my students wanted to be a retail buyer in New York. He was a sharp, well put together young man with great style. On the day the college's career fair, he showed up in a suit by Hugo Boss, leather slip-on dress shoes, cuff links, the works. He was impressive, to say the least. The young man introduced himself confidently to the hiring director for Belk's Eastern division but didn't get the job. People don't always recognize when you do something right, but they rarely fail to notice when you do something wrong, and my student had decided to not wear socks. He wanted to make a bold statement. Unfortunately for him, the hiring manager stated to me later that socks were just part of the uniform. He had made the wrong impression through his non-verbal communication.

I will never forget working with one young lady who was having a particularly difficult time. She was barely five feet tall, pregnant, tattoos everywhere, a multitude of piercings, and living in the homeless shelter. She was determined to put herself through college but was having a rough go of it because no one would hire her.

What she needed was a paradigm shift, a change in thinking, and as shallow as it may seem, she also needed a makeover. Obviously, we couldn't get rid of the tattoos, but we did pick outfits that covered most of them. We also removed the piercings. We purchased a new interview outfit, skirt, and blouse from the local thrift shop. She looked like a different person.

We did our resume work, and it was time for her to try again. The young lady, who had not gotten a second look previously at any of the places she had applied, walked into Hardee's with her new look and retooled resume and was greeted by the manager. He literally asked her if she was 'looking' for a job. Why? She looked professional and confident!

"Yes, sir," she replied, "I was just looking to see if you needed any help."

Since I don't go on interviews with my students, I wasn't there to see how things progressed. However, I was attacked by her in the local grocery store shortly thereafter. "Holly, Holly," she screamed from several rows over as she ran toward my buggy, "I got hired, I got hired." She was so happy. There we were, this short little tattooed pregnant girl, her very large boyfriend, and me, standing in the aisle hugging and trying not to cry. We must have been a sight as everyone was staring at us doing our happy dances.

She explained that the manager was short at least two people, and he inquired whether she had ever worked in the foodservice industry. She told him that she had, so he had her fill out an application hired her before she left the store.

Now I realize that changing one's appearance may seem like selling out or giving up the 'real' you. I assure you that it isn't. This amazing young lady still had her tattoos, she still had her piercings, everything that made her, well, her. However, because she chose to dress appropriately for an interview and the work environment, she now had a job! A job that would help get her out of the homeless shelter, through college, and onto a better life. Again, Amazing!

When you are going through rough times, it's an incredible opportunity to see things in a different light. It is so tempting when other people are unemployed to think, 'why can't they just get a job?' Yet, when you hear the things that these people can truly do and have done, you wonder how they can be unemployed?

It's because life happens, and it isn't always fair, and sometimes it leaves you unemployed... but not unemployable. If you have faith and keep moving, you will find yourself doing your own 'happy' dance in the grocery store soon.

Put 'er there pal: The handshake, a real handshake, signifies acknowledgment, and that is a sign of respect. People like and deserve to be respected, especially employers. Sadly though, the art of the handshake has been all but lost in our culture. Perhaps, we can blame it on technology with all the hands-free devices and social media where relationships are more virtual than physical, but whatever the cause, it's a sad thing.

Were you aware that there are studies that show a good handshake is equivalent to spending three hours with someone? Wow, huh? Okay, I don't fully understand that fact entirely, but I do know that a good handshake makes an excellent impression on people. It makes them feel good about you and themselves, and that is good for business.

A proper handshake is solid, firm, but not painful, thumb to thumb and palm to palm. It also comes with good eye contact. Most importantly, all handshakes should be the same. Women should be confident enough to shake hands with a man, and men should not shy away from offering the same firm handshake to a woman that they do with another man. It's respectful.

But what if it gets weird? Since handshaking is a lost art, there can be some uncomfortable encounters. The rule of thumb is much like the story of Goldilocks and the three bears, it needs to not be excessively short or inordinately long. Since you are the applicant, take the initiative to begin the handshake but allow the potential employer to determine the duration. You will feel them let go. For some, it is a natural instinct to want to wipe away the handshake once it has concluded, you know what I am talking about, you've done it. Resist this urge!

You see this reflex when young children are forced to kiss their great aunt Edna goodbye. It's a brutally awkward moment that leaves the 6-year-old frantically trying to brush away germs from their lips. It may be natural, but it's insulting to the person that you shook hands with, so bite your bottom lip and carry on.

Smile and wave boys, smile and wave: I am originally from Pennsylvania where the sun doesn't shine, and the people don't smile a lot. There is a direct correlation between sunshine, happiness, and smiling people. Everybody smiles in Hawaii because it's always sunny! It's also by the ocean, and most people are on vacation or honeymoon, but I still think that it's mostly because of the sunny weather.

Smiles are the emotional equivalent of sunshine. When people are smiling, the weather is good, bright, and full of potential. When someone isn't smiling, we look for rain!

I know that some of us enjoy a good storm under a tin roof from time to time, but no one really likes 'bad' weather. We see an opportunity on clear sunny days to hit the yard and work in the garden, or grab lunch and set out by the lake, or go fishing with the kids. We like sunshine, and we like people who smile for the same reason. We see potential and opportunity for 'good' things in them. We like having sunny people around, and that is true for employers as well.

Now some people seem happier than others. We call these people extroverts, and they can smile at a funeral. They see the best in everything and everyone, and there is little that gets them down. Yet, if you aren't a Miss Suzy sunshine, all is not lost; you can learn to smile in your own way.

In fact, most men don't smile with their teeth. They smile with their eyes. If you notice, they lift their eyebrows when they are happy, engaged, and 'smiling.' If you are someone who doesn't smile with your mouth, that is okay, just as long as you are smiling with your face!

Did you know that when you are smiling, your voice has more energy? You go up a whole octave, which means that you sound better. It puts color in your voice, and that is far better than monotonous mumbling.

Everyone knows that smiles are effective when we are face to face, but not everyone is aware that you can hear and feel a smile over the phone. Sure, you can! We've all gotten that phone call where the person on the other end sounds like their dog was just swallowed by a hippopotamus. You know the tone of voice that extracts the response, "darling, what's wrong?"

In contrast, you can tell immediately when someone calls with good news! It's in their voice; you can hear them smiling. Nod your head if you know what I am talking about. However, most people never think to 'smile' during a phone interview, but it makes a difference.

I had a client who had his 30-second commercial and resume in front of him when he started his phone interview. He also posted signs all around him that read, 'Smile!' He literally took pictures of it to show me how committed he was to get it right. That was so great!

Have you ever heard the phrase service with a smile? If you smile often enough while you are shopping, people will assume that you work there, and that's what employers value. A smile makes you appear approachable, it sets people at ease, and it makes you more desirable.

Chapter Ten Key Points:

Beyond the Resume Tips:

1. Body Language is important.
2. Dress for Success.
3. Your handshake makes an impression, make it a good one.
4. Don't forget to Smile.

Chapter Eleven

Acing the Interview

The best predictor of the future is the past. This is why the interview is so vitally important. The interviewer gets to really see what you are like, what you have done, and access your knowledge, skills, and ability. I want to make sure you are prepared for the interview.

You may have heard some of the horror stories about people who, while being interviewed, took phone calls or texted, brushed their hair, or even brought their lunch and ate it during the interview. One of the things I realized is that common sense is not common anymore. I realize you wouldn't do any of these things, at least, I hope not.

In case you are not aware of some of the major job No-Nos let me mention 25 according to US News and World Reports, March 2010.

1. Arriving Late.
2. Lighting up a cigarette or smelling like a cigarette.
3. Bad mouthing your last boss or employer.
4. Lying about your skill/knowledge/experience.
5. Forgetting the name of the person you're interviewing with.
6. Wearing sunglasses or a Bluetooth earpiece.
7. Failing to research the employer in advance.
8. Talking about salary or benefits too soon; before an offer is given.
9. Being unable to explain how your strengths and abilities apply to the job in question.
10. Failing to bring your resume or forgetting what you wrote on your resume.
11. Being unprepared to answer standard questions.
12. Failing to make eye contact.
13. Bringing along a friend or your mother.

14. Becoming angry or defensive.
15. Speaking rudely to the receptionist or anyone in the company.
16. Sounding desperate, too familiar, or joking.
17. Chewing gum, tobacco, your hair, your pen.
18. Slouching, yawning, or lip-smacking.
19. Overexplaining why you lost your last job.
20. Checking the time.
21. Leaving your cell phone on.
22. Failing to make a strong case for why you are the best person for the job.
23. Failing to listen carefully to what the interviewer is saying or interrupting.
24. Not dressing appropriately for the interview.
25. Failing to ask for the job.

Remember, you only have one chance to make a first impression, so be prepared. Make sure you know where you are going so you are NOT LATE, **15 minutes early is on time.** As soon as you pull into the parking lot, the interview begins. You never know who is looking out the window, so don't leave your McDonalds garbage outside your car. Be respectful, professional, and personable to everyone you see. That includes the security guard, janitor, secretary. Everyone matters, no one is more important than another person. Everyone matters and has value. Don't forget to SMILE. People hire people; people they like, people they can see themselves working with. If I am an employer and I just interviewed three great people, but I only have one job, and their skills, experience, and knowledge are all about equal, then I want feedback from others. I might go out and ask my secretary what they thought of those three candidates. If my secretary tells me that one of the candidates had a bad attitude or was rude. Guess what, now I am down to two candidates.

One of my clients told me about an interview they had at a Distribution Center. He shared with me that he wore a suit for the interview and took several copies of his resume. He said he was the only one wearing a suit for the interview, the other candidates had on khaki pants and a polo shirt, one guy had on jeans and a polo shirt, another, jeans and a t-shirt. When I asked who he was interviewing with, he told me the President of the company. He was dressing out of respect for the person he was interviewing with, not for the position he was interviewing for. He proceeded to tell me an amazing story. He shared with me that the office manager came and got him and walked him down the hall to a room. When she opened the door, he realized it was the janitor's closet, and there stood a chair. She asked him to take a seat, and they would be right with him. My client said he sat there for what seemed to be an hour but was actually only 15-20 minutes when the door finally opened, here comes the janitor carrying a bucket and mop. He said when the guy saw him sitting there, he started to laugh and said, "You must be interviewing with the President, that's what he has been doing to people lately." My client smiled and introduced himself to the janitor asked him a few questions and found out he had worked there since the Distribution Center opened. He said he practiced his 30-second commercial and shared with him why he was there. After about 20 minutes, the janitor wished him luck and said he had to go back to work. Another 20-30 minutes passed, and the door opened, and the office manager thanked my client and told him they would be giving him a call. When he said, "I thought I was to interview with the President of the Company." She responded, "You just did." You see, the culture of that particular company was that if you thought you were too good to talk to the janitor, then you probably would not have fit in. Also, people often say things to people that they don't think matter. Everyone matters!

Another instance was a client who had an interview with a Financial Firm, and they had about 50 people in suits, all waiting in a large conference room. These folks had all been waiting for over an hour. Finally, the first 10 people were called back, then about 20 minutes later another 15 people were called back. Here, the first 10 people were plants from the company. They were designated to sit among the candidates and determine if they were good fits for the company. The next 15 people were people the plants determined could go ahead and go home. Imagine how embarrassed those people were as they walked by the people they were bad-mouthing the company to now that they had their company nametags on. Make sure you are ALWAYS FRIENDLY AND PROFESSIONAL. There were people that just thought they were talking to a fellow interviewee. In fact, one guy told the company plant, "Yeah, I'm only here because my old lady nagged me into coming. I hear they don't even pay that well."

How to answer interview questions. Most questions today are behaviorally based, that means they want you to give an example. The question will often sound like this: "Tell me about a time when..." The employers want specific examples so they can determine what you are truly capable of. So often, when someone asks, "Tell me about your strengths." And an interviewee says, "I'm a hard worker." I'm sorry, but that is a poor response. Everyone says they are a hard worker; you have to quantify that response. Let me give you an example: instead of just saying you are a hard worker, you say, "While working at NACCO in production, I took it upon myself to get cross-trained in various areas so I could be used whenever they needed me. I took pride in the fact that I was the "go-to" person if they ever needed someone on another line; they knew they could count on me." This response not only shows hard work, but initiative, trustworthiness, and an ability to learn and cross-train.

Let me introduce you to the S.T.A.R. theory of answering interview questions effectively. The "S" stands for "Situation." In other words, describe specifically where you were working. "I was working for BB&T in Richmond, VA." The "T" stands for "Task;" what was your position or job. "I was a financial analyst."

The "'A" stands for "Action" or "Ability;" they want to know what the problem was and what action you took or what skills or ability you used to solve the problem. Example: We had a customer that had an outstanding bill that was about to go to collections. My job was to determine how I could help the client understand the importance of paying the bill and their options on how to pay it. The "R" stands for "Results." Example: I was able to find out that the client's mailing address had changed, and the bank did not have the new information. By updating the client's information, we were able to get invoices to her in a timely manner, and all outstanding accounts were paid. The client thanked me for my positive and respectful manner."

The best predictor of the future is the past. When you are able to answer interview questions by giving specific examples, employers are better able to determine your capabilities. If you handled something capably in the past, most likely, you will be able to handle things in the future.

The Magic 7

Although there are hundreds of interview questions out there, I can tell you after doing career consulting for 20 years, I have found that if you have specific examples in the following 7 areas, you will be able to answer almost any interview question.

1. Leadership
2. Teamwork
3. Communication
4. Problem-solving/ Conflict management
5. Above & Beyond
6. Goal/ Achievement
7. Weakness

The first 6 areas all fall into strengths. In fact, if an employer asks, "What is your strength?" No problem, you already have an example in your hip pocket because you have identified the best examples from your career past in those 7 areas. So now you can say, "One of my strengths is Leadership." Let me give you an example (Now using S.T.A.R. Theory). When I was working at BB&T, I took it upon myself to...) finish the story. I suggest that you write out all 7 examples, stories, whatever you want to call them. The reason you write them out is once you write it, you'll commit it to memory. Then share the examples with a trusted friend so you can practice what you are going to say. Often, when you start practicing with others, you'll remember another example that might be even better than the one you are currently using.

The Weakness question. Please don't be alarmed. I'm about to give you the formula of how to answer the "Tell me about your weakness" question. Are you ready????? You begin with, "My weakness WAS......" Past tense. We want to identify something that used to be a weakness, how we have improved upon it, and how it is now a strength. Here are some examples;

A Manufacturing Manager said, "I used to think I had to do everything myself if I wanted it done correctly. But I learned early in my career, it takes a team to get a job done well. So I learned to delegate and communicate effectively. I quickly learned that I didn't know everything, and you're truly only as good as those you surround yourself by, so invest in others."

I had a young nurse call me and ask me to practice her interview questions with her before her phone interview. When I asked her, "What is your weakness?' She stammered, made sounds like Ugh, Umm, Hmm... she had NOT written down an example, and when it came time, she was not prepared. In fact, this is what she said, and remember, this is a Nurse. She said, "I guess my weakness is I have a hard time finishing things." WHAT???? Oh my, does that mean, "Sorry, Mrs. Smith, I forgot your medicine." She gasped and said, "NO, that's not what I meant." The problem is you can't take an answer back, you only get one chance to make that first impression. After, she composed herself, and we began again. After thinking and writing down her response, she answered the weakness question this way: My weakness WAS, I used to have a hard time saying "No." I like to please people, but I had to learn to prioritize my time to get everything done. I still want to help, but I make sure I get my work done first." That is a completely different response and will create a much more favorable outcome.

Practice:

One of the keys to success in interviewing is practice, so I encourage you to take the time to write out these 7 specific examples using the S.T.A.R. theory. Be sure not to memorize answers verbatim; the key to interviewing success is simply being prepared for the questions. Here are some sample behavioral-based interview questions, and you can see how you can incorporate the 7 examples that you have already developed to answer any of these questions.

- Give me a specific example of a time when you used good judgment and logic in solving a problem. (Problem- solving example)
- Describe a situation in which you were able to use persuasion to successfully convince someone to see things your way. (Leadership or Communication example)
- Give an example of a time when you set a goal and were able to meet or achieve it. (Goal example)
- What is your typical way of dealing with conflict? Give me an example. (Problem-solving/Conflict Management example)
- Give me an example of a time when something you tried to accomplish failed. (Weakness example or Above and Beyond example)

Be prepared to ask questions:

The interview might feel like it's all about you, but it's really not. The interview is about how you can help your future boss and employer succeed. It's about finding out what their requirements are and matching up your background and experience with what they need.

Try to look at the interview through the employer's point of view. You want the interviewer to walk away from the interview impressed and knowing YOU are the solution to their problem. You want to convey that you are there to help them succeed.

Here are 10 questions you can ask the interviewer, so they know it's about you helping them.
1. If I get the job, what are the key accomplishments you'd like to see in this role over the next year?
2. What do you believe are the most important qualifications needed for this position?
3. What's one thing that's key to this company's success that somebody from outside the company wouldn't know about?
4. What keeps you up at night? What's your biggest worry these days?
5. What would make a STAR employee in your eyes?
6. I am very interested in the position. What's the timeline for making a decision? When should I get back in touch with you?
7. How does this company/ my future boss do performance reviews? How do I make the most of the performance review process to ensure that I'm doing the best I can for the company?
8. How did you get your start in this industry? Why do you stay?
9. What's your (or my future boss') leadership style?

10. How is information/ training shared? How do I get access to the information I need to be successful in this job?

After the interview:

Send a typed 'thank you' letter, handwritten card, or professional email within a few days to the interviewer(s). You will also want to re-express your interest and even briefly summarize your strongest qualifications for the position.

If you are not contacted within the specified time, call to restate your interest and inquire about the status of their hiring process. Do not contact the employer if the hiring process timeframe has not passed.

Most importantly, keep NETWORKING. Don't put all your eggs in one basket. If this is the only job you are looking at, you will drive yourself insane waiting for the phone call. Do yourself a favor and keep talking to people to find out what the needs are out there and who you can help! Secret #4 & #5.

Thank You Letter

Example

(Date)

Mr. Kevin Swain
President
Swain Associates
3092 Monte Villa Drive
Tech City, NC 58889

Dear Kevin;

I want to thank you very much for interviewing me yesterday for the **Maintenance Technician** position.
My enthusiasm for the position and my interest in working for Swain Associates were strengthened as a result of the interview. I think my education and experience fit nicely with the job requirements:

- Strive for continuous improvement to maximize production and equipment.
- 20+ years of successful experience in troubleshooting and repair.
- Obtained certifications in Hazardous Waste Training, Safety, OSHA 9000, & OSHA 14,000.
- Maintained and repaired Heating and Cooling Systems, which include Boilers, Air Compressors, Chillers, Vacuum pumps, and Fire pumps.
- Hold a perfect record of attendance.

I'm sure that I could make a significant contribution to the company. I look forward to hearing from you. In the meantime, if you have any questions or I can help in any way, please call me at (123) 456-7777.

Sincerely,
Joe Smith

Chapter Eleven Key Points:

Interview Tips

1. Being early is being on time.
2. The Interview begins as soon as you show up in the parking lot, so be professional and kind to everyone you meet.
3. "People Hire People", so be personable as well as professional.
4. Use the S.T.A.R. theory to answer interview questions (Situation, Task, Action, Results).
5. Remember the "Magic 7"
    i. Leadership
    ii. Teamwork
    iii. Communication
    iv. Problem-solving/ Conflict management
    v. Above & Beyond
    vi. Goal/ Achievement
    vii. Weakness
6. Practice!!!
7. Ask good questions, be interested.
8. Send a thank you.

Chapter Twelve

The Power of Networking

PEOPLE HIRE PEOPLE

Everybody's got a cousin in Miami: Not literally, but we all have connections, relationships, friends, and family that populate our daily lives. We also all know that one person that seemingly knows everyone. You know the guy that you can't pop in and out of Walmart with because he always seems to be running for mayor, shaking hands, and kissing babies.

My point is that you don't have to be gregarious or the life of the party to be an effective networker. All you need is one or two key connections because it's not who you know but who THEY KNOW that often makes the difference.

Here in the south, the saying goes something like, "Yeah, ya know Martha, she's Bill's wife's third cousin; Charlie's younger brother's wife. She was at the church supper last November. Sat right next to 'er. Brought that casserole nobodied eat. That was her."

The point is that we have 'doors' to a great deal more people than we realize when we start seeing things properly. "Holly, I don't like to use people." You are not using people; remember, you have something to offer, and you are trying to identify who can use your help. Please understand, you are looking for INFORMATION, not help! You don't need help; you are offering HELP! Relationships are doors, and if your job is on the other side of that door, then I suggest that we get quite comfortable with knocking and developing our network.

Build a Network: Networking can be a systematic, methodical exercise, at least at first. What you must do is make a list of the people (family, friends, acquaintances) that you already know. These we will label your 'A' contacts. These, in theory, should be the easiest to work with because they are 'hot' contacts. They already know you and probably have a favorable impression of you if not love you. However, it is often these very people that scare us the most because we don't want to damage the relationship. Remember, people want to help people, and that is especially true for those that care about us.

Remember **Secret #5**, 80% of the jobs out there are not gotten through postings. So it is vital that you get in front of the people that have hiring authority before a position is posted. The Directors, managers, supervisors, and owners of companies, they know who is leaving, who is being promoted, fired, etc. way before the position is posted. I am about to show you how you can get in front of almost anyone. First, we have to think about who we can talk to, so we are going to develop a "Contact Grid." Remember, we are NOT asking these people if they know about a Job or who is hiring, we are asking them for INFORMATION of who they may know who does what we do or needs what we do. We are brainstorming with people. So often, people will say to me, "Holly, I don't know anyone." That is a LIE. Everyone has contacts. Life would be impossible without them. Your existing contact network may not contain decision-makers in our career field, but a few carefully selected people from this list will be useful in building your Career Network:

Developing your Contact Grid:

- Friends/ Relatives _____

  _____

  _____

- Former Employers _____

  _____

  _____

- Neighbors _____

  _____

  _____

- College Alumni/Associates _____

_____

_____

- Realtors/Insurance Agents _____

_____

_____

- Hairdresser/Barber _____

_____

_____

- Parents of your children's friends _____

_____

_____

- Professional Associations _____

_____

_____

- Clergy/Faith community members _____

_____

_____

- Doctors/Dentists _____

_____

_____

Networking involves requesting information and expanding your circle of contacts. Now that you have identified people who you can talk to, ask for a small favor: some time, some information, some advice. Almost everyone is willing to give you a few minutes of their time, as you are just looking for advice.

How do you go about developing your network? We drag out our 30-second commercial and start talking to the people on our Contact Grid. You would be surprised at how many of your daily connections don't have an accurate assessment of what you do or have done. It is important that you try to get in front of these folks. 87% of communication is non-verbal, and when you get in front of people, they come up with ideas or people that they might not have thought about if they were just talking to you on the phone or by email. Then when you get in front of them, tell them you are wanting to brainstorm with them, because you are currently looking at several opportunities (Secret #3). But before making a decision, you want to find out what the needs are out there so you can "Help" (Secret #4). Let them know from the beginning you want them to think about who they might know who does what you do (Secret #5). You are trying to identify a NAME. Not necessarily of a decision-making person, although that would be great, but someone who at least gets you closer to talking with a decision-making person.

You might ask why you have to do your 30-Second commercial with people who already know you. They know you through your kids, your spouse, your time at church, but they never see the 'working' you. They don't know that you've spent 6 years as the shift leader at Hospice or that you have your degree in Graphic Design. If they did, they might tell you about their friend Tim down at the printing company where they have their church programs done, he just lost his designer last month and is desperate to find a replacement.

It doesn't cost them a thing to share information with you, so honestly, you aren't asking for much. I had one friend who would always start the conversation, "I need some advice," and then he'd tell them what he needed and end by saying, "I was just hoping you could point me in the right direction." People loved to help him because they wanted to be the person who 'knew' things!

Once you get a name from the "A" contacts, the people you are comfortable talking with. Then you move on to the "B" contacts, they are people that you have never met before, but you have been given their name by someone you both know. Again, let me stress, you are not contacting them because you are looking for a JOB but rather looking for INFORMATION. If you say you are looking for a job, people will not talk with you because you NEED something, and they already have a negative connotation about you before they find out what you have to offer.

I have had 1000s of people that have secured positions by this method. Now you might say, "Holly, I am a professional. If someone came to me and said they were just looking for information, I wouldn't talk with them." That might be true, we are all busy. However, let me point out that if your best friend told them to talk to you, you would make the time to talk to them. The power in networking is determined by WHO SENT YOU.

Three Ways to Ask for an Informational Meeting:

Here are three ways to ask for an Informational Meeting once you have been given a name by your "A" contacts.

- **The "Jane Doe suggested I call you" approach.**

    The referral approach is usually the most effective.

    "I was speaking with Jane Doe the other day, and she suggested that you would be an excellent person to talk to. I am just looking for some information, and Jane said you would be a great resource. Do you have 15-20 minutes next Wednesday or sometime next week?"

    Note: Make sure you give a specific time and have your calendar ready. If you ask for a vague "sometime," I can promise you might not get a time, or it might be in a month or two.

- **"Wanting to talk to an expert in the field" approach**

    "I am about to make some important career decisions and would like to talk to an expert in the field. Your insights and experience could be very important as I make this decision. I would only need 15-20 minutes of your time.

- **"Research current needs" approach**

    "I am currently looking at several opportunities, but before I make a decision, I am doing some research on what the needs are (in your area, or in your industry). I was hoping to set up a time to meet with you next week, I only need 15-20 minutes of your time."

    Let me emphasize again, people hire people, so it is imperative that you get in front of people: NETWORK.

    Also, people are more likely to talk with you if someone they know suggested it.

Everybody's cooler online: Without a doubt, the internet can be a black hole for productivity. I think everyone has sat down with the intention of getting some serious work done only to find themselves scrolling through funny dog videos and wondering how they got there. Yet, for all of the pitfalls that come with the internet and social media, it can be an awesome tool for your job search and career.

First, you have access to a large audience. Sure, not everyone is paying attention to you or is in any way concerned about your wellbeing, but you might be surprised who will lend a helping hand. It is not unusual to have online friends who have real jobs like being a police chief, principle, or restaurant owner.

More notably, there are social media websites built strictly for networking like **Linkedin.com.** In fact, the Wall Street Journal says if you are NOT on LinkedIn, you don't exist (professionally speaking, that is). The US News and World Report state the best way to find a job, 1) Who do you know that knows someone, 2) LinkedIn. Yes, that's right folks, this is a powerful networking tool! This site helps people to get to know you and what you do or are capable of doing professionally. It is incredible! It allows you to start engaging in conversations with people who have the potential to connect you to your next opportunity. This format isn't about the suit and tie, it's about doing research and putting your 'skills and abilities' out there in cyberspace. In short, it's research and networking packaged neatly together.

I know networking is out of most people's comfort zone, so let me share a thought and a story with you.

You will not move until you are more uncomfortable with where you are than with what you have to do.

One gentleman that I worked with had been out of work for over a year and a half. One day, he burst into my office, beaming and smiling from ear to ear with excitement. This was new because this man had a great deal to be stressed over. He was unemployed with no insurance and was a diabetic. Life was hard, and he had been slow to embrace the need to network… until the point in time that he was about to lose his house. Then he began shaking everyone's hand.

His situation had become more uncomfortable than his fear, and he started acting on the information that he had learned. It worked! He made a connection and got an interview.

There he was in my office, a new man. "It was the job I wanted," he exclaimed, arms waving. "I'm so excited. I know this is it. The interview was between me and two other people. I just know I'm going to get it. I'm the perfect fit!"

The next week he is back in my office, lip dragging on the ground and a little black rain cloud hovering over his head. He didn't' get the job. He was just devastated.

He's so devastated that he started to cry in my office. It's not as rare of an occurrence as you might think in my line of work, which is why I keep a stock of Kleenex in my desk. I handed him a tissue, "Holly, I just knew I was going to get that job. I was the perfect fit. I had all the skill sets," sob, sniffle, blow.

The more that he talked, the angrier that he became because he was upset and crying in my office. "I'm going to write to them and find out what I did wrong, Holly."

I'm thinking, 'Oh yeah, that's going to get their attention,' and I suggested that he may want to rethink his strategy. "But I really want to know," he said.

"I know," shaking my head slowly, "but first of all, if there is one position available, and you have three really good candidates, that means that two really good people are going to go home. Period. That is the reality. But if you are doing this, and you are networking, then there are other people who are going to need what you have to offer." It wasn't what he wanted to hear, but, in every way, it was the truth. However, we did end up writing the hiring authority of that company a letter. A "Didn't Get the Job, Thank You Letter." Check it out:

Didn't Get the Job, Thank You Letter

Example

(Date)

Mr. Kevin Swain
President
Swain Associates
3092 Monte Villa Drive
Tech City, NC 58889

Dear Kevin;

Congratulations on filling your sales position. With so many qualified applicants out there, I am sure it was a difficult decision. I really appreciated the time you took to talk with me, not only about the position but about your company. I have to admit, after much research, I was extremely impressed with Green Heck products and solutions. As you pioneer product solutions in unchartered markets, continue to expand and grow, please keep me in mind. I believe I would be an asset to your organization in the future.

- With 20+ years in manufacturing, leadership, and technical ability, I understand the importance of bridging new product design for manufacturability, process development, transition to production, and process control in organizations.
- I believe my demonstrated ability to balance the high urgency required for the manufacturing team to keep quality products rolling under the pressures of rapid growth , as well as the ability to organize technical groups to analyze and solve multiple problems, would be an asset to you as you continue to grow.

> Thank you again for taking the time to meet with me. Please let me know if there is anything I can do for you in the future. I would love to contribute and be a part of such a solid, growing organization.
>
> Then you can add:
> P.S. I have attached my resume for future reference.
>
> Best regards,
>
> Joe Smith

I know, right? Who knew that there was a thank you and congratulations, I didn't get the job letter? Still, it was a good company, and my client really did want to work there. So in the letter, he expressed all of this by saying, "Congratulations. I understand you filled the position. I know it is hard when you have so many good candidates. I was very impressed with your company. Again, I can do a,b,c, and d, so if there is anything I can do in the future, please let me know."

It wasn't long after that the company had another position come available. Who did they think of first? They had already interviewed him and liked him. They had his application, they had done his background check, and even more impressive, they had seen how graceful he was with disappointment. Guess who got the job? Guess who got a better job with more pay than the one they gave to the 'other' guy? Guess who was happy? It's experiences like this that make me love what I do.

He had to get out of his comfort zone and embrace the process under some extreme pressure. My hope is that we can get you moving long before things get so bad for you... but even if they do, remember, there is Hope!

Remember my story? I was brand new to town. I knew no one, not even my neighbors, so when I was thinking about who does what I do or could use what I do, I picked up the phone book! So when you say, I don't know anybody, I understand. I didn't have a professional development class offering me job search information or letting me cry in their office. I turned to the yellow pages and found June Miller's name under Counseling and thought, she's a counselor, I called her.

"June, I'm Holly Sweat. I just moved into the area, and I would love to talk to someone with your expertise who could tell me about the counseling needs in Cleveland County. I was wondering if I could have 15-20 minutes of your time next week?" I gave her my 30-Second commercial but emphasized it was HER expertise I was looking for. I wanted INFORMATION, not a job. In other words, it was not a threatening phone call. She said yes. Really!

So you see, I'm not just the teacher, I'm a *Secrets to Landing Your Next Job* member. It has not only worked for me, it has worked with 1000s of others. I had to network just like I am asking you to do. June was my "A" contact, but then she gave me 3 names of people that I might want to talk to. When I called them to set up an informational meeting, they saw me, not because of me, but because of June!

In fact, one of the names I got was with a counselor at Gardner-Webb University. I had just moved from Atlanta, GA, so I was not familiar with Gardner-Webb University. As luck had it, Gardner-Webb was only a mile from my house. My twins were about 2 years old at the time, so working close to home would have been ideal. However, the meeting with the counselor did not go as expected. After thanking her for taking the time to speak with me and assuring her that June Miller spoke highly of her, I began asking her about the counseling needs at Gardner-Webb. Unfortunately, her responses were very short, guarded, and almost defensive. Oh no, this was so awkward! After asking her a couple more questions, I realized this interview was not going well at all. I found myself looking around her office so that I might find a common bond for us to talk about when I noticed she had a little girl. I asked her about the precious little one I saw in the picture, and her demeanor immediately softened. I shared with her that I had boy and girl twins. However, any more information addressing the counseling issues at Gardner-Webb was no longer on the table. At the end of our brief meeting, I thanked her and asked her, "If you were in my shoes, who would you talk to who does what I do." Nothing, no names, end of conversation.

Fortunately, the next two names that June gave me led to several contacts, and one actually led to a position. Yes, a position. I was talking to one of the "C" contacts, and when I asked them what their needs were and told them about what I had done, they immediately said, "You are exactly what we are looking for." I will also tell you the job that I was offered was one I had actually applied for. This manager, however, never saw my application or resume; it had been lost in the black hole of "online application." But now I was in front of THE HIRING MANAGER, she knew what she needed, understood what I had done and how it would meet the needs of her organization. **Secret #5.** Please note, the reason I was in front of the hiring manager was that I was given her name. She welcomed a meeting with me because of the person who sent me.

This is important, please pay attention. You NEVER want to burn a bridge. Although I ended up getting a wonderful job with EAP in Gastonia, NC by networking, it was in the next town about a 45-minute commute. Not ideal when you have 2-year-old twins. However, two years after working at EAP, I received a call from the counselor at Gardner-Webb University. Yes, she called me out of the blue. She shared with me she was moving out west to go to Divinity School, her position was going to become available, and she had thought of me. The reason she thought of me is that I met her IN PERSON, and we connected, and it ended up a positive encounter because we talked about babies. Here is another important point, when I went and interviewed for the counseling position at Gardner-Webb University, they were so impressed that I had worked with so much business and industry and realized I could meet another need that was not even posted yet, and that was the Director of Career Services. I became the Director of Career Services for Gardner-Webb University for 11 years. I was not ready for that position 2 years earlier; I believe God was preparing me for this next opportunity.

Information with Application Leads to Transformation!

Knowing the power of networking is not going to do you any good unless you actually apply this information. I cannot tell you how frustrating it is to talk to people who have learned this information but then do not APPLY the information. I would ask them, "Who have you been talking to?" Their response is, "Well, I don't know anyone." WHAT????? Look at your Contact Grid! This model of Networking has PROVEN RESULTS.

So let's make sure again you know how to apply this information: We call and get in front of the people on our 'A' list and give them our brief 30-second commercial and then say, "John, you know who I am and what I do, do you know anybody that does what I do or that needs help?" John will start singing like a canary if he has any information, so have a pencil ready. Now all the names that the people gave you from your 'A' list are now going to be referred to as our 'B' contacts. You see where this is going?

Look at earlier in the chapter. You have 3 ways to set up an informational meeting, so you know what to say. Don't be afraid. What I want you to keep in mind is that if you passed them in Walmart, they wouldn't recognize you, so why do we care if they respond poorly to an unsolicited phone call? Besides, you aren't cold calling them, after all. John gave you their name and recommended them to you, remember? So when you call and introduce yourself, the first thing that you are going to say is, *"I was talking with John Smith the other day, and he suggested that I talk with you. I am looking for some information, and John said you would be a great resource."*

Now, they may be the person that you need to talk with, and that would be perfect. However, what you really want is for them to give you a suggestion, another name. These names will make up our 'C' contacts. Another name means another door to network with, and eventually, hopefully, sooner than later, we are going to knock on the right door and find the employer who is 'looking' for us.

The summer before I got to Greenville, I had already made at least one contact, the woman who hired my husband. She was the General Counsel for East Carolina University. You're right, that's a nice title, so I reached out to her. She knew who I was because she had hired my husband. I knew using her name would help me get in the door with people I wanted to talk to.

However, this wasn't my first rodeo. I had plowed new ground before, and it was hard, so I was proactive this time. I had done my research and had three 'informational interviews' set up before we even moved. I scheduled them for weekends when we were visiting the area. I emphasize that these were *informational interviews* over coffee or lunch. I needed a job, but I wasn't looking for a job to come out of these interviews. These interviews are to gather information; thus, we call them informational interviews. Got it? Moving on then.

I had a list of people that I wanted to speak with because I knew that they did what I do, and if anyone could use my help, it would be them, or they would know who did. So my targets included the President of Pitt Community College, the President of the Chamber of Commerce, and someone who worked with Leadership Development at East Carolina University.

None of these people knew me from Adam. They were, in fact, 'C' contacts on my networking list. Dan, my husband, had been my 'A,' and Donna, the General Counsel at ECU who hired him, was my 'B' contact. There were 3 people I wanted to talk to when I contacted them, and they agreed to meet with me because they knew Donna. A couple of things I want to point out; I asked Donna to help me set up these informational interviews or at least to give these people a heads up that I would be calling them so they would be receptive to meeting with me. Please note what a HUGE MISTAKE it would have been if Donna had reached out to these contacts for me for the purpose of a job. If she had contacted the President of Pitt Community College and said, "Hi Dr. Massey, we just hired Dan Sweat to be the attorney for the Brody School of Medicine, and his wife Holly is looking for a job, can you talk with her?" That would have set me up for a disaster! However, she made it clear that I was just doing research and wanted to talk to some experts in the community about the needs in Pitt County, and as a favor to her, would he mind giving me 15-20 minutes. Do you see the difference? Also, I realized the President of an organization does not usually do the hiring for various departments within their organization. It is the Directors and VP's of Departments that determine what positions they need and who they want to hire. But believe me, when I called on people and told them the President gave me their name, they gave me their time. Thus, the power of Networking.

After meeting with each of them, I came away with even more names. One person suggested that I speak to another and so on and so on. Honestly, it can get confusing very quickly, so I kept a list of names kind of like an organizational chart. Remember, I said building a network is a systematic, methodical process, and it's good to keep notes and use a similar contact grid like I showed you earlier in this chapter.

I never asked any of these people if they knew of a job. Instead, I introduced myself and asked them about their organization, which I had already researched, so as to have something to talk about. I asked intentional questions so that I could let them know specific information about me that could help them understand me better and how I might be a help to them.

What I did ask was, "If you were in my shoes, who would you talk to?" Most of the time, I would hear, "Oh, you might want to talk to so and so." Remember that you shouldn't be talking to just anybody, you should be talking to people who do what you do. You're looking to find the employer who needs what you do, and when you find them, it's cover letter and resume time!

Avoiding rejection: The brilliance of this networking model is that you are interviewing people, they are not interviewing you. The premise is you are looking for information, not a job.

When you are talking to your contacts via email, put the person's name who suggested them to you in the subject line.

We are far more likely to open an email if we see a name that we recognize.

In the body of the email, I suggest something like, "I was talking to 'contacts name,' and they gave me your name. I am looking for some information on (subject), and they said that you may be a good resource." If they don't respond to your email, which I had a few of those myself, still try to stop by and visit them. Remember that they have been recommended to you! There's nothing wrong with being in the neighborhood in your suit with a resume. Sometimes they will even ask you if you have one like everyone doesn't carry a stack with them. Geez.

Perhaps the best part of this informational interview contact building approach is that these new contacts will often become active participants in your job search. They have met you, like you, and have an emotional interest in seeing you succeed.

The Key to the Next Contact: It's all about them! They have what you need; they are the experts, the ones in the know and have the connections, so we meet them whenever and wherever it is convenient for them.

When you get a hold of these people, keep in mind that you are only asking for that **15-20 minutes,** nothing more. They will probably ask why you are requesting a meeting; you would do the same, so just stay calm and don't panic. Most people, not all but most, will be flattered that they were recommended and that you are interested in what they know. People are pretty simple that way.

"I am new to the area (or I am finishing up a degree in education) and was looking for some advice on the local school system. (Contact name) suggested that you would be a great person to speak with, and I was hoping to maybe get 10 minutes of your time," is a great response. In that brief statement, you let them know that you value their wisdom and their time and that they have a good reputation with their peers. Does it work 100% of the time? Nothing works 100% of the time, but it does work more often than not.

Remember, you are interviewing them, they are not interviewing you, so come prepared with solid questions about the subject that you are inquiring. This will not only make an impression on them and secure useful information for you, but it will also give you the opportunity to put forth your potential without it being all about you.

Not to belabor a point, and it should go without saying at this juncture in our journey, but always dress appropriately. We should know that you get one shot to make a first impression, and these people may very well hold the key to your immediate future, so let's impress them in a positive manner.

Also, bring your resume. If I were you, I'd think of it like your American Express Card and never leave home without it. It would make me happy if you felt naked when it wasn't with you.

If you build it, they will come: They are going to call you back, and it will probably be while you are in the checkout line at McDonald's, so you need to be prepared. When it does happen, don't panic, just stick to the script, "_____ said you would be a great resource. I am just looking for information. Can I have 10-15 minutes of your time next week?" Remember to designate a time frame, don't just leave it open-ended or it will never happen.

They will probably ask for some more information. You will tell them that you are interested in learning more about (subject) and that you were told they were the right person to see. You just need some advice. This will unlock the door most of the time, and they will agree to meet you at a certain day, time, and place, so make a note of it! I can't tell you how many times we forget the details of a conversation almost as quickly as we hang up the phone. These are details that you don't want to forget. Plus, it would be a good idea to make sure that the date is available for you before making the commitment. The last thing that you want to do is cancel the informational interview.

Pardon me, do you have the time? As sure as the sun will rise tomorrow, you will inevitably have someone tell you that they just don't have the time. It is natural to feel the sting of rejection, but let's refrain from being dysfunctional. There's no need to go into that 'Oh bother, thanks for noticin' me. I'll be in the car, alone, crying' place and walk out dejected.

You know that you are a good employee. You know how hard you are willing to work to be successful. You know the value of your skills, abilities, and experience and what kind of an impact that you can make for an employer. So when you hear someone say that don't have time to see you, and it will happen, try using this reply. "I realize you're really busy. That's why I'm only looking for a few minutes of your time. I can't tell you how much it would mean to me to get your advice." However, the key is using the name of the person who gave you the contact in the first place. Believe me, when I give someone a name, I am counting on them talking to the person, not because of the person I am sending, but out of respect to me.

Will it work? Yes. Every time? No, but it won't work 100% of the time that you don't try it. So go ahead and give it a shot.

To be completely transparent with you, when June gave me those three names, not a single one of those folks wanted to see me. They allowed me to see them because of their respect for June. When you mention a name that they know and like, it creates an instant bond. It stands to reason that they know, like, and respect the person that you mentioned, and therefore, they want the feeling to be mutual. Second, if their mutual friend likes you and recommended them, then it is in their best interest to give you an opportunity. We are wired that way!

"Oh, you know so and so," they say with a great big smile (you're in) "Well, what can I do for you?"

They don't really want to see me, but I get to see them, and that's all that matters.

Be Ready to Be Persistent:

It's not unusual for a potential contact to be proactive, "Sorry, we don't have any openings right now." This is an attempt to dismiss you, and you can let it happen. But every batter gets three strikes, so why walk away after the first one?

"I really appreciate that, but I'm really just looking for information. It would mean a great deal if you could point me in the right direction." Persistence is key to getting the best things in life, so don't give up too soon.

Do you ever follow up with people you've had informational interviews with? Absolutely! Just because someone doesn't have anything right now doesn't mean that they won't have something later. If you've done your work and made a good impression, then it's a safe bet they will remember you when they do have a need.

The nice lady that I met at Gardner-Webb, who had nothing available, thought of me when she decided to change jobs and recommended me for her position. Two years after I met her!

How many times have you heard someone asking at work, "Do you know anybody that would be good for this position?" When this happens to someone you've done an informational interview with, their first response should be, "You know what, I met somebody."

"Holly, I don't know that I can put myself out there for that kind of rejection." That's really what it comes down to, isn't it? What happens when they say no? Nothing, nothing life-changing, anyway. My question to you would be, what if they say yes? Something life-changing!

I read about a man named Jia Jiang, who did an experiment on rejection that was absolutely fascinating and enlightening. At the age of 30, he was a marketing manager for a Fortune 500 company and lived in constant fear of rejection. He had great ideas, but he never had the confidence to succeed. He was afraid of rejection!

So he googled 'how to overcome the fear of rejection' and stumbled upon a website about *rejection therapy*. After doing some research, Jia decided to embark upon his own experiment and started a video blog documenting his quest to be rejected 100 times. Day one, his challenge was to borrow $100 dollars from a complete stranger. In this case, it was a security guard at a large office building. He didn't get the money. However, since his goal was to be rejected, he was successful.

His list included such things as planting flowers in a stranger's yard, teaching a college class, and requesting a burger refill at a restaurant. The funny thing is that even though his requests were sometimes strange and always made to strangers, not everyone rejected him. People literally wanted to help. If you are struggling with rejection like everyone else, take a few minutes and look up Jia Jiang's TedTalk that is posted on Youtube.com. You will be glad that you did.

Be Gracious: Every act of kindness or opportunity offered by others deserves a thank you. If someone takes your call, meets with you, gives you an interview, or even sends you a 'dear applicant' letter, it is important to take the time to say thank you. First, it is just good manners, and that makes a strong impression on people, just remember the gentleman who got the better position because of it. Second, and just as importantly in our job search, it is that it keeps our name in front of important people. People who eventually will have a need that we can possibly meet, and we want them to remember us. So take the time to send a card, email, or make a short phone call to tell them how much you appreciated them making time for you. It may also remind them to pass your name along to someone else.

Chapter Twelve Key Points:

Networking Tips

1. No one lives in a complete vacuum; we all know someone who knows someone.
2. Everyone is a door to someone else.
3. Remember, when networking, you are looking to get an informational interview... not a job.
4. You are searching for something so be intentional, be prepared, and be respectful.
5. People want to help... let them know that your intention is to see who you can help.

Final Thoughts

Where Can You Make a Difference?

IT'S NOT JUST A JOB.

It's so Hard to Say Goodbye: As we close, and I will miss you, I want you to consider something else. I truly believe that God has a plan for you. He has a purpose for you based on your skills, abilities, and experience. So many times, we find ourselves questioning not if God can do it, but does He want to do it for us. Let me assure you, He does want what is best for you. Jeremiah 29:11, *"For I know the plans I have for you, declares the Lord, plans to prosper you and not to harm you, plans to give you hope and a future."* I know that our confidence can be shaken, and our self-esteem can become battered by life's circumstances. However, we are not defined by our circumstances. You have value!!! Remember, negativity is natural, positivity is powerful.

I hope you have found the information in this book helpful. I have been blessed to work with so many amazing people who have implemented the strategies and the Secrets I have unveiled in this book. I want you to know you do have VALUE! You have been given gifts, skills, and abilities for a purpose. I pray you discover your purpose and strengths then begin the process of identifying who does what you do and who needs what you have to offer.(Secret #5) You can make a difference and it can start today.

You see the value of anything, or person for that matter, is really in the eye of the beholder. What one person might throw away is another man's treasure they say, because one sees value, and the other doesn't. Often, we fail to see our true value, but God never does.

Like any good father, God truly wants the best for you, and this is important because family connections are in our 'A' contact list. If God is your reference, if He is the one opening doors for you, then it is safe to say that this job-seeking journey is going to go well for you. Life, in fact, is going well for you once you fully recognize how much He cares for you. (John 3:16)

We are all here for a reason. We all have a purpose, something that we are supposed to do with our lives. I have a wonderful friend who says, "I don't believe in coincidences, only God-incidences." I like that. I believe that you taking the time to read this book is just that, a God incident, and my prayer is that it will not only be a turning point in your career but in your spiritual life as well. I have prayed for you and will continue to do so from this point forward. I am expecting God to bless you richly!

Living in Victory not defeat,

Your friend,
Holly

RECOMMENDATIONS

Ruth Cooper
Healthcare Consultant

Holly is a very motivational speaker with vast knowledge and experience in navigating through the maze of employment opportunities. Her classes provide you with the tools and knowledge needed to successfully find and win that perfect career. Her great sense of humor and practical information are refreshing and also very helpful during a stressful time in your life.

Gregory Morrison
Clinical Analyst at Universal Consulting Service

As a professional navigating the rough waters of "job search," I found Holly Sweat to be a guiding beacon in my efforts to stay on course. Thanks to Holly, my resume is updated, my interview/presentation skills are more focused and effective, and my confidence level is thru the roof. In addition to the invaluable information Holly provided, I picked up many pointers from her delivery, which I found to be professional, polished, and inspiring.

Lori Nease, CPC

President, NEASE PERSONNEL

I've been in the staffing/ placement industry for over 26 years, and I sent my son (who is just entering the work force) over to Holly's workshop. He left feeling positive, confident and ready to manage his job search!

Nancy Cameron-Hubbard
Clinical Analyst Nurse at LENOIR

Holly was a great influence and inspiration to me during my quest to find a job after many years in the workforce. With her tutoring and support, I was able to acquire a new position, boosting my confidence in myself along the way. Her positive attitude and grounded suggestions were instrumental in my progress throughout the interview process, taking the time to coach me through an interview and providing multiple suggestions to make the process go smoothly. Again, thanks much, Holly!

Genevieve Long, PA, MSHS
Neurosurgery – PA UC Riverside School of Medicine

I found Holly's classes to be full of usable knowledge, pearls of wisdom, and an openness to share setbacks, challenges, and success. In her classes, we apply skills needed for the next step in landing a successful job.

I recommend her classes to those who are looking for a job and those who are in transition for a better career. See you at her next class "Secrets of Landing a Job". Genevieve Long

Gus Benson, MBA, BS,HR, SHRM-SCP
Passion for and experience in managing organizational change in several venues.

My job had been eliminated due to downsizing; I was not let go for cause, but it made little difference because I no longer belonged somewhere. I sent off a parade of applications, but nobody seemed to be watching. Holly's two classes (Blunders and Secrets to Landing a Job) took me by surprise. It was not droll speechmaking. Holly is bright, animated, personal, humorous, and is "armed with enthusiasm." "You are special; look at what you have to offer! You are not unemployed, you are looking at several opportunities," she would say to us. Holly was the same outside of class; she was and is enthusiastic and much like a coach always wanting her "students" to win. When I told her I had been hired, Holly expressed her joy at her student finding his way through a rough spot to the other side.

Lynell McDowell
Benefit Resources Special Projects Coordinator at Towne Insurance

Holly is an angel from above. I took both classes "Overcoming Job Seeking Barriers & Blunders" Secrets of Landing a Job," & they helped me immensely in my search for new job opportunities. It is time well spent, & if you implement the tools she teaches, you will be amazed at the results. She is a true professional & awesome at method of teaching, & you will have so much fun while you in her classes!

Allen Spicer
iOS Developer at Capital Bank

Holly is an incredible speaker and motivator. She is a fearless advocate and a welcome companion for many who are in the most critical and vulnerable transitions of their lives.

Linda Butler
Customer Service / Office Administration / Senior Advocate--

Holly Sweat has an incredible talent to motivate people. The reason she is so effective is her multi-level, listening skills that work powerfully in conjunction with her assessment abilities. Her students find her relevant and genuinely invested in their success. Her training modules quickly identify weaknesses and provide empowering model that are do-able. She is amazing

---

Jane Mehringer
Career Coach | Workforce Consultant | Corporate Trainer | Employee Engagement Strategist | All Around People Promoter

As a speaker, Holly takes you on an inspirational and motivational journey. She is wise and endearing and speaks to people on a level that they take away positive tips on how to "Live & Learn, Crash & Burn." I would see her again and again, consistently taking away new strategies and insight on living, she's phenomenal. Thanks Holly!

Renee Bingham
President at God Speed Ministry, Inc.

Holly is a captivating speaker. She shares God's heart with those who need to hear His words of love and encouragement in their trials. Holly's gift of words and humor bring life and light into the lives of her listeners. I highly recommend her as a motivation speaker and as a Christian conference speaker.

Lisa Ritz
Grants Writer, Technical Communicator, Advocate, Trainer

I am currently taking Holly's class "Overcoming Job Seeking Barriers and Blunders." This course is very helpful in navigating a career change, understanding your professional strengths, and being able to go after that dream job! I would highly recommend this class. Lisa Ritz

Kristy Maynor
Human Resources Manager

Holly is a dedicated professional with an uplifting personality. I would highly recommend Holly to anyone who is seeking employment or thinking of a career change. She is truly passionate about the individual she is coaching. Her encouraging, supportive and positive attitude make her an excellent career coach.

Katie Wohlman
Assistant Dean of Students and Director of Career and Professional Development at Lenoir-Rhyne University

Holly Sweat is one of the most positive and energetic speakers I know! She is obviously at home in front of an audience, but she has the ability to make you feel like she is having a private conversation with you while speaking. A very genuine and warm personality, Holly shines in the spotlight, behind the scenes, and everywhere in between! Katie Wohlman, NCACE President (2012-2013)

Sam Leonard Beck
Professional Development Director | REA Career Consultant

Holly is one of the top professionals in the career field in North Carolina. She brings her work ethic, leadership, vision, positive attitude, and strong connection with people to everything she does. Holly's enthusiasm, knowledge, and experience make her workshops and presentations a learning event that is life-altering. Holly Sweat exceeds expectations at the highest level.

Darryl Crawford
Grant Writer / Planner / Analyst

I met Holly shortly after moving to Cleveland County. Not only was I new to the area, but I had been battling a medical disability for nearly two years. I initially contacted Holly to sign up for job search services and training with Cleveland Community College's Workforce Development and Career Services program. What I found was a consummate professional who took an individual interest in the success of all her clients. Her amazing energy and positive outlook were very encouraging to all of us in the program. I have worked with a number of other agencies and, by far, I got the most value from Holly and her associates. I will be starting a new job soon, and I attribute much of my ability to secure the position to the job search skills I learned from participating in the Workforce Development and Career Services program

Todd Hammel, MBA
General Manager at Kloeckner Metals Corporation

After a very successful career, I found myself displaced and back in the job market. A friend of mine recommended that I speak to Holly about my situation. I met Holly to review some of the career development tools she teaches at Cleveland Community College and was simply blown away. Holly has a vast knowledge base and incredible skills when it comes to career development. It was the best investment I had made in my career in quite a long time. I highly recommend Holly

Pamela Pruitt
Marketing and Advertising Professional

You'll laugh....you'll cry.... you'll be inspired by the Christian Motivational Speaker, Holly Sweat. This vivacious woman will touch your heart, as she reveals the difficulties throughout her live and God's love. You'll go home with the blessed reassurance that God is always in control.

Lloyd Williams, Jr
Visionary Entrepreneur and Business developer

Holly takes a real interest in the people she works with. She is a high energy motivator. Holly is a very detail-oriented person and is very knowledgeable of the subjects she teaches. Holly is a true asset to any organization. I look forward to working with her again. Cleveland County is very fortunate to have someone like her.

Karen Ellis
DSS Director at Cleveland County DSS

As Director of Social Services in Cleveland County, I wanted to take the opportunity to enthusiastically endorse Holly Sweat as an exceptional Motivational Speaker. Holly recently provided my entire DSS staff with an uplifting motivational speech at our 2012 DSS Staff Appreciation Luncheon. Holly was able to encourage, motivate, and show appreciation for my DSS staff that make personal sacrifices each and every day as they help those who are less fortunate in our county. She delivered her speech by using personal examples from her own life so that my staff could personally relate to her. She instantly engaged my staff with her energetic, humorous, and humble manner. My staff were uplifted and felt very valued after having the privilege to hear Holly speak. She has the natural ability to engage all types of people and has a genuine love for enhancing the life of others. Her compassion, energy, humor, and sincerity make her an outstanding motivational speaker. I highly encourage you to utilize Holly Sweat for your next event if you want to re-energize your staff.

Joel Okon
System Support Engineer at Teradata

In 2009, I left the printing industry to pursue an education in the IT field. I enrolled in the computer information program at Cleveland Community College, and upon graduation, needed a resume to reflect my new skill set. I signed up for Success: Land Your Next Job to accomplish this goal. Holly helped me craft a dynamic resume that quickly generated responses from prospective employers. They also gave me the tools to successfully navigate the interview process. Although I had no direct background in the IT field, I did possess skills developed from over 25 years of employment. With Holly's coaching, I was able to relate my talents to the qualities employers sought in their candidates. I landed a job with a great company, and I wouldn't have been able to do it without taking this class. Holly and Jack have a passion for helping people, and I highly recommend Success: Land Your Next Job to anyone seeking an opportunity in today's job market

Patricia "Darlene" Robertson
CNC Machine Operator at Eaton

I was apprehensive about taking a class to begin with, because it was about creating resumes and interviewing techniques. Something I didn't think I would gain much from.

Boy oh boy, was I wrong! Holly kept the class entertaining, upbeat, and interesting. She taught me so much about the transferable skills that I have and how to present them to potential employers. I could tell that Holly honestly cared about each and every person in class and wanted us all to be the best that we could possibly be in the field that we choose. Whether we were staying in our field of experience or transferring to a new field as I was doing. As a single parent of two children, I had a variety of work experience but didn't know how to communicate efficiently the skills that I had to offer. Holly was very helpful in showing me how to handle interviewing with potential employers as well as tips on finding potential employers with the economy in the shape that it is in today. I was able to land the first job I interviewed for after taking the class. One of my interviewers told me that I had the best answers to his questions that he had ever had during an interview. Yes, I was still nervous, but I blew them away with the way I was able to present myself & my skills during the interview. I started work the very next day! I know I would have fumbled my words had Holly not prepared me. She made a world of difference in my interview.

Leslie K. Wright
Career Counselor | Resume Specialist | Student Affairs Professional | Job Search Strategist

I have been professionally connected to Holly for the past 12 years through the North Carolina Association of Colleges and Employers (NCACE). She is a joy to work alongside, and she continues to be a role model for me. As a leader, Holly exhibits strength and confidence while inspiring growth and action of her team. As a coach and a counselor, she is simultaneously empathetic and directive; a delicate balance, indeed! I highly recommend and endorse Holly Sweat for her work and expertise in career and life coaching/counseling and leadership.

Jack Weller
President, North Carolina Lutheran Men In Mission Start second year - focus is on change & how it will help our ministry

Enthusiastic, Encouraging, Patience, Listener, Willing to Go the Extra Mile -- these qualities are apparent during your first few minutes in a seminar or talking one on one with Holly. She truly is there to help you develop a strategy to continue your career. Taking advantage of new technologies such as LinkedIn, Career Builder, and other social networking options, she encourages you to be pro-active and approach finding your next opportunity the same way you approached your previous job. Her success is all about relationships. Holly enthusiastically supports your use of Informational Interviews that point toward someone in an organization who is the decision maker for new positions or the hiring manager. As you share your efforts, she is listening, suggesting, offering helpful hints to keep you focused on your goal. When you think that there is nothing else you can do, Holly offers encouragement, suggestions and one on one help to build your resume, refine your interview skills or aid in the mining of past experiences to find that gem that will lead to success. I am pleased to recommend Holly as one who will make a difference.

AWARDS

Holly M. Sweat recipient of this year's Dupont Davis Award.
Holly M. Sweat is a seasoned workforce development professional with extensive experience in counseling, consulting, motivating and teaching individuals to overcome barriers to make successful careers. Upon acquiring her Master's Degree in Counseling Psychology from Indiana University of Pennsylvania in 1984, she started her career as a licensed clinical therapist for various entities until being hired as the *Director of Career Services* at Gardner-Webb University from 1998 to 2008. Holly was hired as the *Director of Workforce and Career Development* at Cleveland Community College from 2008 to 2014. Holly started working at our local community college as a Human Resource Development Instructor in 2014.

Holly is a professional leadership and workforce development trainer who started her own consulting business, called *Hope Motivation and Success*, in 2007 and has been contracted by numerous businesses, corporations, and government organizations to develop and implement organizational improvement strategies toward improving services, in addition to motivating leaders and employees to achieve their goals. Holly continues to present leadership and workforce development speeches and presentations at local, state, and regional conferences and workshops.

When Holly began working for Pitt Community College in 2014, she brought all of her experience and unique approach to teaching highly effective career development classes with her. Almost immediately upon being hired, she visited Neal Anderson at the NCWorks Career Center in Pitt County to collaborate and work toward preparing our job seekers in the mechanics of effective job search strategies and techniques. Her dedication to our clients and all NCWorks staff and partners, in addition to her positive attitude, has positively impacted our mission and has prepared thousands of our job seekers in acquiring effective job search strategies and techniques.

THANK YOU !

Thank You For Reading My Book!

I really appreciate all of your feedback, and I love hearing what you have to say.

I need your input to make the next version of this book and my future books even better.

Please leave me a helpful review on Amazon letting me know what you thought of the book.

Thank you so much!
Holly Sweat Raper & James Jennings

www.ingramcontent.com/pod-product-compliance
Lightning Source LLC
Chambersburg PA
CBHW060417220526
45465CB00008B/2923